Praise for *Restore*

I like to visit prisons, hospitals, and recovery centers—it is there that the truth is evident and people are without pretense; attention is given and change occurs. While you may never get to go to rehab, in *Restore*, Vince will take you there. In his book, Vince gives you care and concern and gracefully coaches you toward honesty and action. If you are ready to face your issues and knock them down, then read *Restore* and your life will be changed.

KYLE IDLEMAN
Pastor; author of *Not a Fan* and *Grace Is Greater*

Vince Antonucci is a talented writer and dedicated leader who has helped so many on the road to healing. *Restore* shows a clear path to overcome the baggage in your life and live free. Such an excellent tool!

JUD WILHITE
Senior pastor of Central Church; author of *Pursued*

I love this book and believe it will lead you and those you love to freedom from issues that keep you in bondage to the past. Vince has not only experienced this in his own life, but he has a front-row seat to watch God set people free daily through his ministry in Las Vegas.

GENE APPEL
Senior pastor of Eastside Christian Church, Anaheim, CA

Restore can be summed up in five words: "You can't . . . but God can." Of course, the value of those five words takes many more words to unpack and process, as Vince does, convincingly, through the lens of going to spiritual rehab. There's a lot we can't do when it comes to our seen and unseen addictions, but there is nothing God can't do when we have the courage to partner with God to confront them. No matter where you're at or what you're going through, pick up the book, start your journey to healing by reading it, and let God take care of the rest, chapter by chapter. You won't be disappointed.

RUSTY GEORGE
Author of *When You, Then God*

Vince has written a fantastic book that helps people break out of the junk that puts them in chains. It's biblical, practical, and will make you laugh! I loved it and think it will help anyone trying to deal with the junk in their past so they can move forward.

BOB ROBERTS
Senior pastor of Northwood Church; author of *Lessons from the East*

Most people have an addiction in one way or another. Those who recognize it and work it through are some of the most genuinely happy, fulfilled, and unstuck people I know. Read this book!

LEON FONTAINE
CEO of Miracle Channel; author of *The Spirit Contemporary Life*

If you feel stuck . . . if you have hurts you can't get free from, self-destructive habits you can't get past, read *Restore*. Vince will make you laugh, cry, and most important, learn how to move past your past!

JOHN BURKE
Author of *No Perfect People Allowed*

Tired of those secret layers of your life that deter you from being all God wants you to be? Vince Antonucci's six-step process peels away the layers and leads you along the road to restoration. Vince shares his personal journey along with biblical truth, allowing you to no longer be defined by your past.

DAVE STONE
Pastor of Southeast Christian Church, Louisville, KY

Restore

RESTORE

break out of your past and into God's future

VINCE ANTONUCCI

TYNDALE
MOMENTUM™

The nonfiction imprint of
Tyndale House Publishers, Inc.

Visit Tyndale online at www.tyndale.com.

Visit Tyndale Momentum online at www.tyndalemomentum.com.

TYNDALE, *Tyndale Momentum*, and Tyndale's quill logo are registered trademarks of Tyndale House Publishers, Inc. The Tyndale Momentum logo is a trademark of Tyndale House Publishers, Inc. Tyndale Momentum is the nonfiction imprint of Tyndale House Publishers, Inc., Carol Stream, Illinois.

Restore: Break Out of Your Past and Into God's Future

Designed by Mark Anthony Lane II

Edited by Jonathan Schindler

Published in association with the literary agency of The Gates Group, 1403 Walnut Lane, Louisville, Kentucky, 40223.

For information about special discounts for bulk purchases, please contact Tyndale House Publishers at csresponse@tyndale.com, or call 1-800-323-9400.

Library of Congress Cataloging-in-Publication Data
Names: Antonucci, Vince, author.
Title: Restore : break out of your past and into God's future / Vince Antonucci.
Description: Carol Stream, Illinois : Tyndale House Publishers, Inc., 2017. | Includes bibliographical references.
Identifiers: LCCN 2017034699 | ISBN 9781496415776 (sc)
Subjects: LCSH: Self-actualization—Religious aspects—Christianity. | Success—Religious aspects—Christianity. | Habit breaking—Religious aspects—Christianity. | Regret—Religious aspects—Christianity.
Classification: LCC BV4598.2 .A58 2017 | DDC 248.4--dc23 LC record available at https://lccn.loc.gov/2017034699

Printed in the United States of America

24	23	22	21	20	19	18
7	6	5	4	3	2	1

Contents

REHAB . . . FOR THE REST OF US

I SHOWED UP FOR my first sex addiction group session with everything I thought I would need: a Bible, a notebook, and a pen.

There was, however, one thing I *didn't* have: a sex addiction.

My Friends' Common Element

I have a friend who started partying in high school. In college he turned to cocaine, and, as it will, the cocaine turned on him. It moved from a party companion on the weekends to his master. He was its slave. But today you wouldn't know it. He hasn't done drugs in years and is a healthy, well-adjusted guy. What happened to him? Rehab.

I have another friend who developed a massive gambling addiction. I'm not talking about losing a few bucks at the weekly guys'-night poker game. I'm talking about owing *millions* to Vegas casinos and bookies and the Mexican mafia. I'm talking about using all his friends for their money and having people threaten to kill him. But he hasn't gambled in years. In fact, he's one of the most stable, reliable guys I know. What happened to him? Rehab.

I know someone else who grew up hearing comments from her mother about watching her weight, that boys don't like chunky girls. Over time she went from hearing those comments to being held hostage by them. Years of bulimia followed. She felt horrible about it and about herself, but she couldn't stop. She tried, but it seemed beyond her control. Today? You guessed it: no more eating disorder. What happened to her? Yeah, *rehab.*

But I've left out an essential part of their stories. It's actually the *most* essential part. The equation that led to their finding wholeness looked like this: God + Rehab = Healing.

They would all tell you they couldn't have done it without God. But they'd also confess that knowing God wasn't enough. They believed in God before becoming addicted, throughout their addictions, and during their failed attempts to change.

It wasn't until they learned and applied the principles God gives us as a path to healing that they moved out of their addictions and toward wholeness—that they finally broke out of their past and into God's future.

Restore

Those friends of mine were *restored.*

What do I mean by restored?

To be restored is to be brought back to the right *place.* Think of a runaway teenager returning to the loving home of his family. He's restored.

To be restored is to be brought back to the right *condition.* Think of a classic car someone is lovingly repairing so it's like new again. It's being restored.

What is it that you and I are really longing for? I believe it's restoration.

We know we're not where we need to be in relation to God. There's distance between us. It may be that we ran away in a full rebellious sprint, or it may be that we unintentionally drift away on a daily basis.

We know we're not where we need to be in our lives. None of us grew up thinking, *I hope someday I'm overweight and not really doing anything about it,* or *I'd like to grow up to be a bitter, unforgiving person,* or *I want to live with a victim mentality so I always blame other people for my problems and never move forward,* or *Someday I want to be in a marriage that's devoid of passion.*

We know we're not where we should be with God or with who we are, and what we desire is to be restored.

It's a theme throughout the Bible. The psalmists cry out, "How long, O LORD, until you restore me?";[1] "Restore to me the joy of your salvation, and make me willing to obey you";[2] "I have suffered much, O LORD; restore my life again as you promised."[3] The prophets plead with God, "Turn me again to you and restore me, for you alone are the LORD my God";[4] "Restore us, O LORD, and bring us back to you again!"[5] The apostle Paul names it as the goal: "Your restoration is what we pray for" and "Aim for restoration."[6]

It's what we need. The good news is that it's what God is offering.

God promises to restore us. He says, "I will restore them because of my compassion" and "I have seen their ways, but I will heal them; I will guide them and restore comfort to Israel's mourners."[7]

The question is *how?* How do we experience God's restoration? It's something God has to do, but we have a part to play. So what is our part? Are we doing what we need to become recipients of restoration? Why doesn't everyone experience it? And, much more personally, why aren't *you* experiencing it?

My Other Friends' Missing Element

That brings me to some of my other friends. Actually, *lots* of my other friends.

I know someone who shops and shops and shops. She doesn't shop for things she needs; she just needs to shop. She keeps buying more clothes, more shoes, and more jewelry, and she hates herself for it every time she receives a credit card bill. She can't stop shopping, because no matter how hard she tries, she can't spend her way out of an emotional hole.

I have another friend who keeps moving. Every two years he packs up his family and heads off to the next place. Ask me, and I'll tell you he's running. Ask him, and he won't be able to tell you what he's running from.

I have friends who want to exercise but can't seem to start and friends who don't want to smoke but can't seem to stop.

I know people who have a constant, desperate need to please their parents and others who are desperate to stop yelling at their kids.

I have a buddy who wants to be a professional musician but always finds a way to sabotage his own efforts and another buddy who sabotages every romantic relationship that has real potential.

I have friends who struggle to maintain a job because they can't stop playing video games and others who are so addicted to their jobs, they can't find time to play a game with their kids.

And all these people I'm talking about believe in God. The issue *isn't* that they lack faith.

So why can't they do what they want or stop doing what they don't want? What's the missing element for them?

Rehab.

My Rehab

My problem was that I couldn't forgive my father. Growing up, I hated him. He was an abusive bully. He launched his demeaning words like heart-seeking missiles, intended to do maximum damage. Occasionally his hands became weapons as well. He punched holes in walls to show his disgust with me. Even as a little kid I suspected that when he wasn't home, he was probably with women who weren't my mother.

When I was eleven, he walked out on us altogether. Later in life I learned it was actually a pattern; before us he had abandoned two other families.

My dad spent most of his life in and out of jail. When he wasn't imprisoned, he would occasionally pop into my life, usually to borrow money to fund his gambling addiction or some scheme he was working on.

When I received the phone call that he had died of a heart attack, the only emotion I felt was relief. Sure, it meant I would never get back the thousands of dollars he owed me, but it also meant I'd never have to see him again.

I was constantly angry because of him. I walked through life simmering. I knew I wasn't healthy and my relationships weren't healthy, but what could I do? One of only two people who were supposed to love me had chosen to hate me. He was supposed to comfort and care for me but had tyrannized me. Of course I was going to be a toxic mess. Of course I would always despise him.

There was only one problem.

I became a Christian.

I was a Christian who loved my heavenly Father but still hated my earthly one.

That would have been fine with me, except I kept running into verses in the Bible like these:

- "Whoever claims to love God yet hates a brother or sister is a liar. For whoever does not love their brother and sister, whom they have seen, cannot love God, whom they have not seen."[8]
- "Make allowance for each other's faults, and forgive anyone who offends you. Remember, the Lord forgave you, so you must forgive others."[9]
- "If you forgive those who sin against you, your heavenly Father will forgive you. But if you refuse to forgive others, your Father will not forgive your sins."[10]

I wanted to go Edward Scissorhands on the pages with those verses, but I couldn't. I had submitted my life to God's authority. I wanted to obey him.

So I decided to forgive my dad. I even said it out loud.

The only problem was that I *didn't*. I don't know if I was lying to God or myself or if I wasn't really lying at all; I just know I didn't forgive him. I still hated him.

A few years later I became a pastor and started teaching people about God's love, while I continued to have revenge fantasies in which I would find ways to hurt my father the way he had hurt me.

I wanted to forgive him; I just didn't know how.

Then I had my first kid. Suddenly, living as a bubbling cauldron of bitterness became a more pressing issue. How would it affect my ability to love, and have compassion for my children?

That's when two of my friends told me about this program for people with sex issues and addictions. They had both gone and said it was perfect for me. I told them that while I had a buffet of issues, sex addiction wasn't one of them. They explained that sexual issues for many people can be traced back to problems with their fathers. The program helped people learn how to forgive their fathers.

Hmmmmm.

The idea of going to a support group for people with sexual issues didn't appeal to me, but I realized that there *wasn't* a support group for people who couldn't forgive their fathers, and I *needed* to forgive my father. So I went.

The facility the support group was held in was about a mile from the church where I was pastor. I was pretty nervous walking in the first night, wondering, *Will anyone driving by see me? What will they assume?*

I also felt uncomfortable when the group I had been assigned to sat in a circle and everyone was asked to introduce themselves and why they had come.

"Hi, I'm Jim. I can't stop looking at porn. Even at work, I look at porn all day."

"Hi, I'm Russ. I use women for one-night stands. I often will have sex with two or three strangers in the same day."

"Hi, I'm Jeremy. I'm married, and my wife doesn't know this, but I'm also attracted to men and have had sexual encounters with them."

My turn. "Hey, guys. I'm Vince. Um, I haven't forgiven my father." (Questioning looks.) "That's it." (Continued questioning looks.) "No, really, that's it." (#Awkward.)

But I kept going. I went every week for twenty-seven weeks. I did the homework. I read the books. I completed the assignments. And by the end of the program, I had forgiven my father. For real this time.

It was powerful. It set me free. And it changed my life. It's now sixteen years later, and I've been bitter-free ever since.

I mentioned earlier that God promises to restore us. I undersold it—God's promise is even better. If God promised *just* to restore us, it would mean that he could help us make our lives what they always should have been. That's great, but there's still the sadness of the life we lost. But check out what God says in Joel 2:25: "I will restore to you the years that the swarming locust has eaten" (NKJV).

Locusts had invaded Israel and ruined years of crops. The fields of the farmers were in seeming disrepair. Yet God promised not only to return the fields to their intended condition, but also to supply what was lost in the wasted years.

That's what I've experienced. I ruined years of my life on bitterness. My heart was bitter and seemingly beyond repair. But God not only changed my heart; he also restored the years I lost, stuck in my unforgiveness. Finally I broke out of the dysfunction of my past and into the freedom of God's future for me.

Why?

By myself, I couldn't do it.

With God, I still couldn't seem to do it.

But God + rehab: *boom*.

Your Rehab

I don't know what you're struggling with. I don't know what you've tried. But my guess is that your problem probably isn't considered "serious" enough for there to be a rehab center or twelve-step program for it.

I'm now a pastor of a church in Las Vegas, just off the Strip. All kinds of ordinary people with all kinds of ordinary problems show up every week. What I've experienced, and what I've witnessed others find, is a God-centric path to healing that happens when we apply the biblical principles people learn in rehab and support groups. In fact, for the past seven years, we've been offering a core course at my church and this past year launched a ministry dedicated to teaching people the principles of recovery so they can move past their past, heal the hurts and self-destructive habits that keep them from freedom, and experience truly changed lives.

I'm guessing that's what you need as well. That's why you're reading this. You don't need a path to healing and wholeness based on *self*-help, or pumping up your *self*-esteem, or developing your *self*-control. You've tried that. You already know that doesn't work. That's why this path isn't centered on *self* at all; it's *God* centric. It's based on the most powerful healing force in the universe: the unconditional love of God.

This path also isn't about behavior modification. Our tendency is to make resolutions and set goals and try to muster up the willpower to start doing what we haven't been doing or to stop doing what we have. We've all tried that, and we know it doesn't work. Our willpower quickly loses power. Not only does it not work, it's not God's way. Jesus chastised the religious leaders of his day, the Pharisees, for focusing on externals. It's *not* about modifying our behavior. God's path is one of healing and experiencing transformation from the inside out.

Reading this book will put you on the path you'd learn about in rehab.

The best way for this book to effectively take you through recovery and toward freedom is if you read, process, and seek to apply one chapter at a time, one day at a time. You don't go through a rehab program in a day. Programs may be as short as a week but are often thirty days. So let this book take you on a deep journey of recovery. In fact, that's why the book has exactly thirty chapters, so you can read, pray about, talk to a friend about, and apply one chapter a day.

On that "talk to a friend" part: What if you read this book in community? Get a friend or a group of friends to read it with. One of the steps in the restoration process is "I stay connected to God and others." By reading this book with a friend, or a group of friends, you'll already be putting that principle into practice. It will also probably make the journey more fun, and I can basically guarantee that having people to talk to, be encouraged by, and keep you accountable will make the results more powerful.

We've created a digital community at TheRestoreCommunity.com for you to connect with other readers and find helpful resources to discuss this book with a friend or group. On the website you will find more than thirty videos that correspond to each chapter in the book as well as a downloadable journal and guide. All of this is completely free.

As you journey through this book, you're going to encounter drugged-out rats, explosive diapers, secrets I never thought I'd share with anyone, the truth about why you put what you put on social media, how I've mistaken prophets for bullfrogs and theologians for root-beer inventors, the time I almost drowned my wife and then she almost drowned me, and a woman who did not get off her toilet for two years.

You're also going to read some silly top ten lists. The journey to a restored life involves some deep soul searching, and it can be painful, so a few laughs along the way might be nice.

Most of all, you're going to discover how to turn to an extraordinary God to find healing for your ordinary problems and how having his transforming love poured into you on a daily basis can set you free and empower you to live the abundant life Jesus promised.

My guess? You'll never be the same.

THE TOP TEN LEAST POPULAR SELF-HELP BOOKS

10. *Box It Up: Why Feelings Are Stupid*

9. *Who Moved My Colostomy Bag?*

8. *Windows XP for Beginners*

7. *Your Marriage Can Be 3% Better*

6. *How to Make the Best of Your Below-Average Looks*

5. *The 7 Habits of Socially Unaware People*

4. *Glory Days: It's Not What's Ahead; It's What's Behind!*

3. *How to Instagram the Life You've Always Wanted*

2. *Making Toast for Dummies*

1. *How to Win at ATMs*

OUR PROBLEM

I don't like to talk about it.

But I know it.

Honestly, I don't even like to admit it to myself.

But I'm pretty sure it's true of you, too.

In fact, "it" has got all of us.

What is "it"?

It's our problem.

We're unique and different in all kinds of ways,

but when it comes to our problem . . .

we're all the same.

THE BLOWOUT

I WAS A FIRST-TIME FATHER. That's my justification for the pee-soaked carpet, my pee-soaked clothes, my pee-soaked hair. Even for the poop on the ceiling.* My wife was out and had left me to care for our baby. Dawson was a couple of months old, and I figured, *How hard can this be?* I told myself, *Men have been taking care of babies when their wives are out for centuries. In fact, men much more irresponsible than somewhat-responsible me have been taking care of babies for centuries.* I was confident. I was ready.

Then Dawson had a blowout.

Let's make sure we have a common definition. A blowout is when a baby goes "number two" with such volume and force that his or her diaper cannot contain it.†

---

* I'm not really sure if there was poop on the ceiling. I do think there *might* have been poop on the ceiling—and in this book, I'm not covering up anything.
† Think Mount Vesuvius but more sudden—and *much* grosser. And instead of destroying an Italian city, a blowout destroys the parents' spirit (and anything it touches).

Dawson had a blowout, and I thought, *I can handle this. After all, babies have been having blowouts for centuries.*[*]

So I began the biohazard cleanup. Taking off Dawson's diaper was relatively easy. The trick was getting his clothes (which had number two on them) over his head without getting any number two *on* his head. I was accomplishing this with a surgeon's steady hand when it started to rain. I found that surprising since we were indoors in my living room. That's when I realized Dawson was going number one, and I hadn't yet put a new diaper on him. Unprepared for that kind of precipitation, I did what any resourceful young father would do: I cupped my hands and caught the number one. Unfortunately, my hands quickly filled, and number one started going wherever number one wanted to go.[†]

About two minutes later I called my wife. "Here is the situation," I told her. "I am in my underwear. Your son is naked. There is number one *and* number two *everywhere*. What should I do?"

She asked, "Do you want me to come home?"

I thought, *Of course I want you to come home!*

But I *said*, "Of course I don't want you to come home. I can do this. But what should I do first?"

If we're going to walk the path of recovery, the first thing we have to do is admit we have a problem.

The truth is, we've all had a blowout. We're all a mess.

The issue is that we don't see it. Or we won't admit it. And that's what keeps us sick.

A problem denied can destroy you. A problem hidden cannot be healed.

Twelve-steppers have a saying: "You're only as sick as your secrets." Let me tell you a secret—they're right.

---

[*] For inspiration, I tried to picture a father having to clean up his baby in the Elizabethan era, wearing a powdered wig and being all, "Thou blowest out thy diaper. Methinks thou hast wrought a plague upon our house!"

[†] I guess number one is called number one for a reason. I can say that, for me, after this day, I no longer question my son's authority.

The Same As It Ever Was

In the story of the first humans in the Bible, the sequence of events is kind of stunning:

God creates Adam.

God puts Adam in a perfect garden paradise.

God tells Adam he can enjoy everything in the world except for the fruit of one tree.

Adam is alone.

God creates a naked wife for Adam.

Adam and Eve get to run around naked and tend to the garden naked and play naked volleyball.

Then they hear a deceptive whisper: "This isn't the good stuff. God is holding out on you."

Somehow Adam and Eve buy the lie that having a perfect relationship with God and playing naked volleyball with each other is not that great—that things could be better if they ate from the tree God told them not to eat from. And so they eat the fruit of the forbidden tree.

Adam and Eve have a blowout. They mess up.

And what is their response? They go into cleanup mode. They hide from God and hope they can keep their mess concealed.

It turns out living in denial doesn't exactly work for Adam and Eve. Soon they're no longer naked, no longer living in the garden paradise, and their firstborn son commits the world's first murder.

Even God's Favorite?

I don't know if God plays favorites. It kind of seems like he wouldn't. But if you read the Bible, it seems like he does. It seems like this guy named David is right at the top of God's list of favorite people.

Who is David?

He is a man who loves God a lot. And yet one of the stories from his life has another stunning sequence of events:

David is standing on his roof.

He sees a naked woman named Bathsheba, who is taking a bath on another roof.*

He sends his men to bring her to him.

He has sex with her.

She gets pregnant.

David, not wanting anyone to know he's the father, tries to get her husband to sleep with her.

When her husband doesn't take the bait, David has him killed.

David has a blowout. He messes up, to say the least.

And his response is to go into cleanup mode. Not only does he try to hide his sin from God and others; he keeps living as if nothing had happened.

Does living in denial work for David? He later wrote, "When I refused to confess my sin, my body wasted away, and I groaned all day long. Day and night your hand of discipline was heavy on me. My strength evaporated like water in the summer heat."[1]

David was as sick as his secret.

Not Me!

The thing about you and me is that while we may not eat forbidden fruit or look at naked people from rooftops, just like Adam and Eve and David, we've blown it. We've had our blowouts. We've messed up.

Actually, let's be honest. It's worse than that.

I recently had to go to a hardware store. I hate going to the hardware store and only do it about once every decade or two. I hate it because I am not handy. That's an understatement. I can't fix *anything* around the house. I have friends for that. I have a wife for that. That may sound bad, but I'm pretty good at writing sermons. And if my friends or wife ever needed me to write one for them, I would do it. What I need from them is to fix the broken drawer, or figure out how

---

* The fact that Bathsheba was taking a bath makes me very happy. If she had a sister named Showersheba who took showers, my life would be complete.

to put together the new lamp, or change the battery in the smoke detector. Seems to me it's a fair exchange.[†]

So I hate going to the hardware store.

The reason I went to the hardware store is because I needed some way to chain up my dog, Kuma, in my backyard.[‡] We have a fence around our backyard because we want Kuma to be able to enjoy the freedom of running around outside without the danger of him getting lost or of a car running over him. But Kuma finally realized he can squeeze between the bars of our backyard fence.

One day I heard him out back barking frantically, so I went out and saw that he was stuck halfway through the fence. He looked up and noticed me, which somehow gave him the motivation he needed to push himself the rest of the way out. Suddenly, he was free, and he gleefully ran around the neighborhood until I finally caught him and brought him back inside.

Later, I let him out again, and he squeezed through the bars again. When I finally found him, I decided not to let him into the backyard anymore. That's when the real trouble started. Now that Kuma has tasted running around outside of the backyard, it's all he can think about. He's constantly at the back door barking. When I won't let him out, he'll come over and sit next to me like we're best friends, then return to the back door and bark. He's trying to create a codependent relationship! He thinks he can manipulate me into enabling his dysfunction! He will do *anything* to escape the boundaries I've set for him.

Here's the deal for you and me: God set boundaries around our behavior because he loves us and wants to protect us from doing things that can get us lost or hurt. But when we go outside God's boundaries, we discover that sinning can be pretty fun.

Most preachers don't mention that because, well, we don't want to feel like we're promoting sin. But we all know it's true. If there were

---

[†] Well, it will be if they ever need a sermon. No one has asked me to write them a sermon yet. But I'm ready!

[‡] Normally such man's work would be my wife's job, but she was out of town for a few days.

no upside to sinning, no one would do it. Think about it. No one feels tempted to rent a hotel room so they can read the Gideons' Bible, or to eat an entire stalk of celery, or to search the Internet for pictures of nuns, or to score a dime bag of Flintstone vitamins. No, people are tempted to rent a hotel room so they can have sex with a prostitute, or to eat an entire cheesecake, or to look at pictures of naked supermodels, or to score bags of weed.

Why? Because sinning temporarily feels good and can be fun. So it's not just that we blow it. We don't just sin. We get *hooked* on sinning. We *specialize* in it.

That's not something we proclaim very proudly. Your résumé probably does not list "Specialist in Sinning." Even so, I bet you have things you know you shouldn't do, and you don't want to do anymore, but you can't seem to stop doing. You may not see it as an addiction, or even a habit, but maybe it is.

The question is, *What do we do about it?*

Me Too?

First, we need to admit we have a problem. What we *want* to do first is anything but.

Just like Adam and Eve and David, we try to keep our sickness a secret. Sin isn't a popular word today. Pretty much the only place you'll see it outside of church is on a dessert menu.* The problem is that a problem denied can destroy you, and a problem hidden cannot be healed.

And we need healing.

I can picture you right now. You're squirming a little. You're thinking, *Not me. I'm not sure I need to read this book. I realize I'm not perfect, but my sins don't rank up there with Adam and Eve's or David's. And this book is about recovery and rehab, but I don't have any addictions.*

Guess what? That's what *every* addict thinks.

---

* I like decadent chocolate desserts as much as the next person. Okay, I like them **more** than the next person.

Addictions like drugs and alcohol are more visible and more socially unacceptable, but we *all* have our addictions—things we couldn't bear the thought of giving up or doing without, habitual ways of thinking or living that aren't healthy. Unfortunately, except for fleeting moments of clarity, we typically don't see them. Ours may not even be a conscious denial. We're just blind to our addictions. As Jesus said, we see the splinter in our friend's eye but miss the tree trunk in our own.[2]

So we live in denial. It's actually easier for us to live in denial than it is for a drug addict or an alcoholic because even if we are aware of our problems, we can deny that they're serious. The Bible says that we should not be enslaved to or mastered by anything,[3] but we can't imagine that applies to the things *we're* obsessed with or controlled by. Our obsessions just seem innocuous and not worthy of being compared to real addictions we don't have.

Except . . . they're really not that different.

That leads to a couple of questions we should probably consider.

First, *what is an addiction?* Basically, it's when a person develops a compulsion to seek something out, loses control in limiting intake of that something, and has a negative emotional reaction when prevented from having that something.

Read that again. Might that describe your relationship with your phone, or video games, or social media, or watching TV, or certain sexual activities?

How does a person become addicted? From a physical perspective, there are reward pathways in the brain that get activated when a person has a pleasurable experience. Sometimes the exhilaration is so pleasurable, the person chooses to do it again.

Unfortunately, habituation—or what some call a "tolerance effect," where the same action produces less pleasure—often comes into play. But instead of giving up on the activity that's giving less pleasure, the person may go back to it, trying to re-create the sensation of the first time. Because of the tolerance effect and habituation, the person needs to do more of the activity, or do it more often, to get to that same experience. It keeps taking more and more sex or cheesecake or porn or weed to feel as good as we did before. You don't need me to tell you the root of habituation: it's *habit*. And soon a habit is a full-blown addiction.

Here's the thing: those same reward pathways that get activated by sex or cheesecake or porn or weed get activated in your brain when you buy a new outfit, or have a revenge fantasy about that person you still hate, or accomplish something that makes you feel successful, or share gossip that makes you feel better than someone else, or look lustfully at an attractive body, or notice someone looking lustfully at your body, or receive praise.

What you experience, and perhaps feel compelled to experience again, is really not that different from someone smoking crack or finishing off another bottle of wine.

So now, when you think of addiction, instead of thinking, *Not me!* perhaps you'll realize, *Oh. Me too.*

The truth is, we've all had a blowout. We're all a mess. And your mess is messing up your life. Denial may help you ignore that, but trust me: denial *isn't* working for you.

All of this makes me think of this one time Jesus met a man who was filled with demons. Jesus asked him, "What is your name?"[4]

Bet you know where I'm going with this.

If you're going to be healed, you have to *name* your demons. No more hiding. No more concealing.

When David finally stopped living in denial, when he looked in the mirror and acknowledged everything to himself and to God, it set him free. He went from "My body wasted away, and I groaned all day long" to "You forgave me! All my guilt is gone" and "You surround me with songs of victory" and "Rejoice in the LORD and be glad."[5]

Real freedom awaits us, and it starts with naming our demons.

But not yet. Our problem actually goes deeper than this basic understanding of addiction. It's much deeper, and we'll talk about it in the next chapters. Then maybe we'll be ready to reveal our secrets. Because we're only as sick as our secrets. And we don't want to be sick anymore.

*   *   *

In all honesty, this is going to be difficult to do alone. We weren't made for it. We'll get into that later, but I want to encourage you right now to read this book with others. We've created a digital community as a place to get started. Join TheRestoreCommunity.com to engage with other people on this journey. You'll find videos to go with each chapter and even a detailed PDF journal that will offer reflection questions, Scripture passages, and helpful activities to help restore you to God and one another.

THIRSTY

IMAGINE BEING THIRSTY—really thirsty—and then getting a drink. Now imagine that after drinking, you find yourself even thirstier. Still thirsty, you start feeling desperate. What do you do? You drink more, but it does nothing to quench your thirst. In fact, you're thirstier still.

Pretty soon you'd realize there was something wrong with what you were drinking.

Heather Kopp was a respected Christian writer. Both she and her husband worked in the Christian publishing industry and faithfully showed up at church each week with their two children.

At church, Heather would worship God. At home, Heather would spend her days drinking alcohol. She strategically planned out her day to make sure she never went long without drinking. Not wanting her husband to know about her addiction, she hid bottles of wine in the boots in her closet. She was pretty much always drinking alcohol, and yet she was pretty much always thirsty for more. She says drinking gave her a brief sense of satisfaction:

> *But for how long?* For a while. *And then what?* I'd want more. *And then?* It would begin to fade, and I would want another drink, another glass. *And then?* Well, more! *But if what you crave is alcohol, then how come it never truly satisfies you?* It was a good question. . . . Where did this deep sense of want and longing come from?[1]

It's easy for me to read about Heather Kopp and question why someone who has God would turn to alcohol. Was it to escape? Was it to find meaning? Why did she keep going back to it? Wouldn't it quickly become obvious that she wasn't finding fulfillment in a bottle? Why didn't she just stop drinking? Why was she an addict?

But . . .

When I was in high school, I would spend hours, sometimes entire *days*, practicing baseball or soccer. I might convince the best pitcher on our team to come out and throw me curveballs all afternoon. Or I would practice dribbling up and down the soccer field by myself. I wasn't trying to make the team. I had already made the team. I wasn't trying to become a starter. I was already a starter. I had to be *the best*.

In ninth grade I scored the most goals of any ninth grader on my soccer team. How did that make me feel? Like I had to do it again the following year.

In tenth grade I scored the most goals of any tenth grader on my soccer team. How did that make me feel? Like I had to do it again the following year.

In eleventh grade I scored the most goals of any eleventh grader on my soccer team. How did that make me feel? Like I had to do it again the following year.

In twelfth grade I scored the most goals of any twelfth grader on my soccer team. How did that make me feel? Like I wasn't sure what to do next because there wouldn't be a following year.

In fact, in one of my seasons I came one goal away from setting the record for most goals in a season in the history of my high school. Do you know how that made me feel? Like a failure.

In college, I decided for the first time in my life to study and get good grades. It turned out good grades weren't good enough; I had to be the best. I studied endlessly, and if a professor was going to post exam scores on a wall, I was at the wall waiting for him. If a professor passed out our graded exams, I would go to him after class to find out if mine was the highest grade. If I got a 98 and someone else got a 99, that felt like failure. It was unacceptable. When I received the highest grade, I didn't feel good or celebrate it; I just turned my attention to the next exam.

After college, I became a pastor. I work endlessly to make my church a growing church. When it grows, I pray it will grow more, and I become frustrated when it doesn't. I spend hours writing sermons, then more hours practicing them so I can give them without notes and seem like I didn't spend hours writing them. I put out books and then keep checking my sales to see how well those books are selling.

I am thirsty. I am *really* thirsty. My whole life I've been looking to success to quench my thirst, but every bit of success I've experienced only makes me thirsty for more.

You'd hope that at some point I'd realize there's something wrong with what I'm drinking.

Wouldn't it quickly become obvious that I'm not finding fulfillment in my achievements? Why wouldn't I just stop trying?

Two Sins

I read the Bible often, but sometimes the Bible reads me. A verse hits me because I realize it *is* me. There's a verse in the book of Jeremiah* that hit me so hard one day, I almost threw up. God says, "My people

---

* Which I later found out had nothing to do with a bullfrog. My mistake.

have committed two sins: They have forsaken me, the spring of living water, and have dug their own cisterns, broken cisterns that cannot hold water."[2]

We are so thirsty. We long for something, and that something is God. Friendship with God, a relationship with him, loving him, worshiping him—*that's* what we were made for, and it's the *only* thing that will quench our thirst.

God is the one who is supposed to comfort us when we hurt and help us get through our struggles, provide joy, and be what we think about and look forward to.

The problem is that we've forsaken God, who is living water, and we're looking to something else.

It could be something pretty *un*healthy and potentially dangerous like alcohol, tobacco, drugs, or gambling. Or it could be something relatively healthy and *not* generally thought of as dangerous, like food, exercise, popularity, sex, shopping, acceptance, or our jobs.

Pastor Tim Keller says the heart of sin is making a good thing the ultimate thing.[3] It's taking something that's fine and putting it in the place of God.

We start looking to this other thing to make us feel good, to comfort us when we hurt, to help us through our struggles, and to provide joy. We find ourselves thinking about it and looking forward to it.

So maybe you come home stressed from a hard day at work, but instead of taking those feelings to God, feeling his presence, and getting a sense of peace from him, you have a glass of wine or spend three hours in front of a TV or cruising around the Internet.

Or perhaps, instead of trying to find purpose and joy through a relationship with God and making a difference for him in the world, you find purpose in partying on the weekends, playing video games, or going to the gym and sculpting your body.

Here's the problem: this other thing we're using cannot do what we need it to do. It may be a good thing, but it is *not* the ultimate thing, and it cannot truly meet our needs. It may make us feel good for a minute or an hour, but it can't give us real comfort, can't truly get us through our struggles, and can't provide lasting joy.

Not only this, but sometimes after this thing makes us feel good for a minute, we end up feeling *worse*. Right? Maybe we feel regret or shame. We've got a hangover, or a credit card bill we can't pay, or kids who resent us because we spend so much time at work.

The thing we're turning to cannot do what we need it to do, and often it ends up just making us feel worse.

Then, when we realize it didn't come through for us, instead of giving up on it because it's not a good God for us, we go back to it, hoping this time it will give us what it didn't last time. There's always the promise *This time will be different*. But it's *not* different, and again it doesn't give us what we need—because it can't.

And we're still thirsty.

Why?

Two sins: we've forsaken God, the spring of living water. And we've dug our own cisterns, but they're broken and can't hold water.

Idolatry

The Bible talks about this replacing-God-with-something-else-that-isn't-really-God-and-can't-possibly-do-for-us-what-God-can-do issue *a lot*. In fact, it's in the Bible more than almost any other topic. The Bible doesn't refer to it as "replacing-God-with-something-else-that-isn't-really-God-and-can't-possibly-do-for-us-what-God-can-do." No, the Bible refers to it as *idolatry*, and idolatry is as natural to us as breathing. We *all* turn from God to idols.

That's why God made the first two of the Ten Commandments against idolatry. We shall have no other gods before him, and we shall worship no created thing. It's why two Jewish scholars argue, "The central . . . principle of the Bible [is] the rejection of idolatry."[4]

Remember those Dr Pepper commercials where people would dance through the streets singing, "I'm a pepper, he's a pepper, she's a pepper"? Well, I'm not sure why drinking Dr Pepper makes me or anyone else a pepper. But if there were a commercial with some dude prancing around a city singing, "I'm an idolater, he's an idolater, she's an idolater," I really couldn't argue with it. I would vote for it as the weirdest commercial of all time, and I would wonder what exactly they were advertising. But I couldn't argue with it.

You may want to argue with it though. Perhaps you've read the Bible, and you think idolatry is when people worship a false god named Baal or salsa dance around a statue or bow down to a log with a face carved in it.

The reality is idolatry is more than lying prostrate before a totem pole. Here's a smart guy's definition of idolatry:

> Anyone or anything from which you and I try to acquire life, value, and meaning—outside of the true God—is a false god. Therefore, those positive behaviors aimed at generating life and acceptability for us are sins. So even though *what* we do may be right, the reason *why* we do it is idolatrous.[5]

So, if I look to anything other than God to find life or value or meaning, that thing becomes for me a *false* god, an idol. These things may not necessarily be what we would think of as "gods," and they're not necessarily bad things. But they are things we put in place of God, and we look to them as our primary source of joy, fulfillment, self-esteem, or security. Your idol could be food, fame, your marriage, a retirement fund, your career, a house, your kids, travel, or (for me) church growth.

Really, the object itself isn't so much the idol as what we do with it. That's why God tells us, "These men have set up idols in their hearts."[6] It's what the thing does inside of us that makes it an idol. When something becomes more important to us than God, more central to our hearts than God, it has become, for us, our god.

Jesus teaches us to seek God first, trusting that the other things we need will be provided for us as well.[7] Idolatry is when we seek something else first.

So, if we're being honest, we all have a problem with idolatry; it's what we do. We may not be peppers, but we are idolaters.

And we're still thirsty.

Why? Because God loves us and made us so we couldn't be satisfied with anything other than him. Nothing in this world will ever be able to fill the hole in our hearts. The Bible says it this way: "He has planted eternity in the human heart."[8]

Do you know what that means? It means you and I have something my dog doesn't.

I told you about my dog, Kuma. Well, Kuma doesn't think about eternity much. He goes out in our backyard* and lays on his belly in the Vegas sun. He likes to play with a tennis ball. He's pretty happy. He never stops and thinks, *Wait a second. Why am I playing with this ball? Is this all there is? If all of life is simply playing with a ball, I don't think I want to live!*

No, Kuma is doing fine. He doesn't have much to worry about, because God didn't place eternity in my dog's heart.

But God *did* put eternity in your heart and in mine. So I can't just lie on my belly in the sun for long. After a couple of minutes, I'm thinking, *I'm going to die someday. Why am I lying out here in the sun? Is this how I should be spending my time? And why do I keep playing with this tennis ball? Have I become obsessed with this ball? What am I doing with my life?*

Why do I think like that? Why can't success be enough for me? Why, after I return from vacation, do I start thinking about the next one? Why is enough never enough? Because God has put eternity in my heart.

And he's put it in yours.

That means only God can satisfy us, because we crave something beyond this world, something longer lasting than the temporal stuff of earth, something bigger than anything we can grab in this life. Unless we make God our God, we'll still be thirsty.

---

* We put up a screen so he can't get through the fence and escape the backyard. When I say "we" put it up, I mean "my wife."

A SAFE PLACE TO HIDE

Brennan Manning was one of the most popular Christian authors and speakers of the last several decades. His book *The Ragamuffin Gospel* exploded in popularity. A ragamuffin is a "shabbily dressed, dirty child," and Manning's idea is that when we look at our good works, at what we have to offer God and the world, well, we're not much to look at. We're just ragamuffins. We try to make ourselves good enough, we strive to keep up appearances, but no matter what we do, we're still just ragamuffins. But the good news is that we're *God's* ragamuffins.

Manning never stopped writing about God's grace for ragamuffins all the way into the last years of his life. God loves us not for who we should be but for who we are. Though we are far from perfect, he loves us with a perfect love. Manning wrote, "My deepest awareness of myself is that I am deeply loved by Jesus Christ and I have done nothing to earn it or deserve it."[1]

Brennan Manning's obsession with how God loves ragamuffins struck a chord, so he continued writing books and was invited to speak all over the world. Night after night he spoke to thousands of people who were desperate to hear good news for ragamuffins, and night after night Brennan Manning was desperate . . . for alcohol. When the crowds went home to contemplate God's love for ragamuffins, the ragamuffin they had just listened to went to his hotel room to drink until he passed out.

Though he battled for sobriety and had moments of victory, from the age of sixteen into his last years, Brennan Manning abused alcohol. And he wasn't an "I might have had one too many" drinker. He was a "woke up in the morning and didn't know where he was, his wife and kids ended up leaving him, he missed his own mother's funeral because he was passed out in a hotel room" drunk.

What drove Manning to drink? Well, it started at a very early age.

His mother was abusive and his father an alcoholic. His parents divorced, leaving Manning to grow up in a broken home. He needed to escape the reality he faced every day. The truth is that every soul needs a safe place to hide. His soul needed a place where it could feel protected from what was out there. Unfortunately, Manning turned to a bottle.

I get that.

I don't drink, but I do hide. We all do, because every soul needs a safe place to hide.

Like Manning, I grew up in a broken home.

There were broken walls, where my father's fist had broken through in anger.

There was a broken piano. My father, in a rage, spotted my mom's beloved piano, which her mother had left her when she died, and broke it to spite her.

There was a broken window. One night one of the people my father had conned for gambling money came by and threw a brick with a threatening message written on it through our front window.

There was a broken spirit. My father had a special skill in making me feel bad about myself. He would call me names, maliciously point out every mistake I made, and always make sure I knew I wasn't good enough.

There were broken promises, like when my father went on another of his trips to gamble in Las Vegas, telling us he would come home soon but then never returning.

And so, like Manning, I was left to grow up in a broken home. And I needed to escape my reality. My soul needed a place where it could feel protected from what was out there.

I didn't turn to alcohol. Perhaps I would have if, like Manning, I had an alcoholic parent.

Instead, I turned inward. I decided I would avoid people whenever possible. I wouldn't care about people or let them care about me. Getting close to people meant getting hurt by people, and I was too smart to let that happen again.

I developed a protective shell, a facade I hid behind, an impostor I showed to the world. My impostor allows me to not show people the real me, the me my father rejected and convinced is unworthy of love and acceptance. By hiding behind the facade, the real me can never get rejected. The world is a scary place. The real me knows that. My soul is fragile. And every soul needs a safe place to hide.

Your Safe Place

Maybe, like me, you hide behind a mask.

Or perhaps, like Brennan Manning, you hide in a bottle.

Or it could be that you escape to a fantasy novel or to your Instagram feed, or that you escape through food, or sex, or shopping, or letting people take advantage of you so they'll like you, or working long hours, or winning competitions so you can feel that you are better than others, or telling lies, or gaining power over people through your anger, or practicing religion.

Can you see how you hide, where you hide?

The world is scary, and life is hard, and we try to escape the negative feelings. Have you ever said, "I need to watch a movie and just escape for a while"? Or been sad and found yourself eating a tub of ice cream? Or been uncomfortable with the way your life is progressing, but instead of dealing with it, you just started playing some mindless game on your phone? Or been unhappy with your husband and drifted into a fantasy world in which you were married to someone else? Or gotten angry at someone and went to the gym to "blow off steam"? Or been guilty and used some kind of religious activity to feel better about yourself? Or been unsatisfied with your sex life with your wife so you turned to pornography? Or you didn't like the way you felt others perceived you, so you bought something for them, or let them take advantage of you, all in the hope that they might like you?

Does that mean you're an addict? Not necessarily. But it does mean that instead of dealing with a difficult reality, you tried to escape from it or to create an alternate reality you could fantasize about living in.

Where do you hide?

What do you use?

Pain Avoidance or Creation?

You may realize that you do this, but you're wondering if it's a big deal. After all, we all need a safe place to hide. Your way of hiding may seem kind of innocuous.

It's not. It's *cancerous*. Because while we all need a safe place to hide, our tendency is to hide in places that aren't safe and that result in greater pain than what we're hiding from.

In my situation, I chose to keep people at a distance and not show anyone the real me. But Jesus said life is all about loving God and loving people. (Thanks, Jesus—that's *exactly* what I decided not to do.) I wouldn't let anyone love me, and I wouldn't love anyone; that way I wouldn't get hurt. I wouldn't let anyone know the real me; that way they couldn't reject the real me.

Then I started to realize that when people told me they loved me,

I couldn't believe them. I would be thinking, *If you knew the real me, you wouldn't love me. You only love the image I project.*

My hiding also poisoned my relationship with God. I didn't know how to be real with him, either. I didn't want to show him any weakness, because what if he hurts me too? And then I felt guilty because my relationship with God wasn't real, but that's what I wanted.

It occurs to me that I don't feel safe with God or anyone unless I appear flawless. So I have this compulsion to be perfect. But I know that what God wants, true spirituality, is not about being right; it's about being *real*. It's not about being competent; it's about being *authentic*. It's not about being impressive; it's about being *intimate*. It's about allowing God and others to be present with me in my messiness, my brokenness, my fears, and my failures. But I can't seem to do that. And then when I do good things, when I'm caring or generous or transparent, I wonder whether it's real or whether it's just another image I'm projecting to impress people, or even God. Which, of course, is crazy, because God knows my heart. He knows what's really going on, so I can't fake him out. The problem is that *I* don't know me. I don't know what's real or fake.

I started living this way back when I was young as a defense mechanism. It was supposed to protect me from pain, but it has caused me far more pain than it ever took away. It has stolen the life I'm supposed to live and replaced it with confusion and guilt and shame.

Can you relate?

Your soul needs a safe place to hide.

The way you try to hide, whatever you use to escape pain—is it causing you more pain than it ever alleviated?

Do you see that it's a problem and that there must be a better way?

Are you ready to go to rehab—for the rest of us?

Me too.

But first I want us to think about our problem in one more way.

PLAYING GOD

I'VE HAD SOME INTERESTING jobs in my life, several of which I was totally underqualified for.

My first job was picking grapes for a winery. I lived in Hammondsport, a little town* in upstate New York with several wineries, and vineyards surrounded my house.

Then I got a job at the Hammondsport Tourist Information Booth.†

Throughout high school I stocked shelves at a grocery store.

In college I worked at a movie theater and a law library.

I was, briefly, a taste tester for Kentucky Fried Chicken.‡

---

* Hammondsport is *very* little. If you ever go to visit, my house is the one on the left.

† Yes, Hammondsport gets tourists. In fact, it was named "America's Coolest Small Town" by *Budget Travel* magazine. I would argue, however, that the town lost all its coolness when I moved away in 1988.

‡ Best job *ever*! I would go at lunchtime to the KFC headquarters in Louisville, Kentucky, and get paid eight dollars to eat chicken and new products. (I had KFC chicken pot pie before you ever *dreamed* KFC might have chicken pot pie.) If they ever start offering that as a full-time job, sign me up!

For twenty of the past twenty-one years I've been a pastor.

The one year I wasn't a pastor, I did stand-up comedy in a show in a Las Vegas casino.*

But there's one job I've been doing consistently all of those years, despite being woefully underqualified. Oddly, I was never offered the job. I just fired the person who was doing it and took over. The position? God.

Don't laugh. You've fired God and taken his job as well.

Job Descriptions

God has a job. I doubt he's the type who makes sure everyone has job descriptions, but if he were, his might read:

Job Title: God

Job Responsibilities:
- Rule over the world
- Rule over each person's life
- Be the perfect heavenly parent of each person

Reports To: No one

And you and I have a job description. Ours reads:

Job Title: Me

Job Responsibilities:
- Trust God
- Serve God
- Be God's child

Reports To: God

---

* Don't be too impressed. The first paycheck I received was for less than ten dollars.

The problem is that each one of us has fired God, and we are not remotely qualified to do God's job. Personally, I can say I'm more qualified to be a brain surgeon, even though I can't change the batteries in my smoke detector. I'm more qualified to lead the New York Philharmonic, even though I can't play an instrument. I'm more qualified to write a book, even though I can't read.[†]

But even still, I fire God and take over. I think, *I've got this.* I'm delusional like that.

In Control

Now that I've taken control and put myself, not God, at the center of the world, I start trying to control everything.

For instance, I try to control my image. If I'm going to play God, I need people to be impressed with me! If I can control what you see of me, then I can control what you think about me.

I've realized that one of the things I do is to try to make people think I work harder than I do. Occasionally I'll count how many hours I work in a week. Let's say I count sixty-six. Well, in a staff meeting the next week or in conversation, I might just happen to mention, "Yeah, I work too much. I counted my hours last week. It was, like, seventy." Why did I say "seventy"? Because it's acceptable to round up? No, because I want people to think I work more than I do so they'll think I'm better than I am. I want them to think I'm more disciplined than I am. I want them to do the math and think, *Wow, he must start working at 5 a.m.!* Because if I can control your image of me, I can control what you think of me.

Some years ago I started eating better and working out, and I lost some weight. One day a friend of mine, who knew what I weighed when I started, asked, "What are you down to now?" I had just weighed myself that very morning, so I knew *exactly* what my weight was, but when I opened my mouth, I told him a weight that was one pound lighter than reality. Why? To control his image of me. *Wow,*

[†] This is probably not the right place for me to admit that.

Vince is doing this right! He is disciplined! He's even one pound lighter than he looks!

See, because I'm trying to play God, I can't let others know that I'm not God, that I'm not what I'm trying to be. So I work to control my image.

I also try to control the details of my life. Why? Because it's my job! I plan out the sermons for my church years in advance. Ask me sometime what I'm preaching any particular Sunday of the year 2043. I know. If my wife would let me, I'd plan out our vacations for the next twenty years. Why? I want to be at the center of my universe, pulling the strings, in complete control.

I also try to control people. It might be that I give someone a compliment. Generally there's nothing wrong with that. But I've realized that sometimes I do it to get something for myself. Or when I text people and they don't respond quickly enough, I'll send them another text that simply says, "??" No response will elicit a third text: "????" I need an answer. I need it *now*. I try to control people. I do it because I've put myself in the place of God, and I'm overseeing the world.

This really gets crazy when I have the audacity to try to control God. I wish I were kidding! For instance, sometimes if I'm in a hurry, I'll be tempted to skip my Bible study and prayer time. But usually I'll do it anyway. Do you know why? Not because I love God and love spending time with him. No, it's because I'm trying to control God. I don't want him to disapprove of me, and I think maybe by doing it, even if my heart isn't in it, somehow God might reward me. Maybe he'll care about me more. I'm trying to control God! I am sick!

Every day, I'm tempted to say, "God, you're fired. I'll take over. I can control myself and my world. I'll be God." And then I start controlling, even though I'm not even close to being qualified for God's job. So I have to work hard at it, and I have to work hard at not letting others see that I'm not qualified to be God.

It would be totally embarrassing for me to tell you all this except for the fact that you do the same thing.

You've fired God. You're overwhelmed trying to do his job, which is why you are controlling. It may look different from how I do it, but you do it too.

You might control your image through social media. You post pictures on Instagram and updates on Facebook that make it look like you're living a perfect life with your perfect family. It's not an accurate reflection of reality, but you're not interested in showing reality. You're controlling what people see of you so you can control what they think of you.

Maybe you try to control other people by giving advice—lots of it—to everyone. You're always telling everyone what to do, whether they want to hear it or not. The advice isn't really about helping them get better; it's about helping you get power.

Or you might control others by taking care of them. Control isn't the motive of every caring person, but it's certainly the hidden motive of some. Perhaps you don't think you have an impressive personality, so instead you make people dependent on you by caring for them. The more you help, the bigger you become and the smaller they seem.

Another way you may try to control is by withdrawing. People want to know you, love you, care for you, but you won't let them. You hold everyone at a distance. You control by withdrawing.

Perhaps you control people with rage and anger. You yell and threaten and scare people into doing what you want. Because you are God. This is your world. How you make other people feel doesn't matter.

Or it might be the opposite. You control people by acting helpless. You're always dropping hints on your Facebook page about how bad things are for you, all the struggles you're having. You play the victim because it keeps others tied to you.

What's our problem? We've fired God, taken his place, and we're desperately trying to gain and stay in control.

We're all suffering the consequences for it.

The Consequences of Playing God

We try to control our images, but there are consequences. One is that we have to tell bigger and bigger lies. We have to generate a bigger-than-life image to impress people so they'll think we're really something.

So one day I'll be at our staff meeting saying, "Yeah, I started working at about two thirty this morning. I'm now working, like, 125 hours a week." Or I'll tell my friend, "Oh, I'm down to about ninety pounds. Yeah. These clothes just make me look a little heavier."

Another consequence of controlling your image is if anyone ever tells you they love you, you can't believe them. You're thinking, *You love the projection. If you knew the real me, you wouldn't love me.* So you end up chronically lonely.

Control isolates us.

It's not just that we're alone—we're afraid. We're afraid of being exposed. Afraid that someone will find out the image isn't true. That's terrifying.

Controlling people also has negative consequences for our relationships. You know why? Because people don't like being controlled. It took me a long time to figure that out! If you are controlling people, people are pulling away from you. Some go away passively, others aggressively. Controlling people always hurts your relationships.

It also has negative consequences for our relationships with God. God will not be controlled. But we try. When we do, God lovingly withdraws. He patiently waits for us to give leadership back to him. In the meantime, as we try to get our way, I wonder what we're missing out on.

There are all kinds of consequences, and they cause us all kinds of pain. They are constant. We don't like pain, so we develop coping mechanisms to manage the pain and make us feel better. These coping mechanisms often become addictions. We endlessly watch TV or movies; we waste time online; we have inappropriate sex; we drink too much or overeat or overwork or lie or gamble or gossip about others so we can feel better about ourselves.

We feel compelled to control. We fire God. And there are constant consequences, so we develop self-destructive habits to manage them.

Not Me?

What's interesting is that Christians are people who have confessed to God, "I'm incapable of taking care of my sin." A lot of us admitted we were powerless to take care of our sins, and we became Christians, but then every day since then we have said, "God, I'm capable of taking care of myself." We gave God control of our eternity, but we fire him daily and take control of our here and now. I wonder if the very essence of sin is telling God to take a hike.

If you don't believe that's true for you, let me ask you a clarifying question: Do you ever worry?

Jesus said people who have God as their Father won't need to worry, and in fact, they *won't* worry.[1] Only people who are trying to be in control worry.

Maybe you can admit you've fired God and are trying to play God. If so, if you're like me, then you've got a problem.

THE TOP TEN SIGNS YOU'RE PLAYING GOD

10. All your pets are in pairs, male and female, and you have *a lot* of them.

9. Whenever you write people notes, you etch them in stone tablets.

8. You purchase a large amount of frogs to wreak havoc on your troublesome neighbors.

7. You have only five slices of bread but expect it to be enough to host a huge Super Bowl party.

6. You go to flea markets just to flip the tables over.

5. When it's dark, instead of just hitting the switch on the wall, you loudly proclaim, "Let there be light."

4. Every time you tell a story, you start with "In the beginning . . ."

3. You give advice to fishermen on where they should cast their nets.

2. Instead of sending an e-mail, you burn a bush in front of someone's house.

1. When correcting your kids, you start with "Thou shalt not."

DIDN'T TRY TO MAKE
ME GO TO REHAB

So you've got a problem and you need help. You're in good company. We *all* need help.

But unlike Amy Winehouse, no one is trying to make you go to rehab, so you don't have to say, "No, no, no."

But does that mean you don't need it?

Estimates are that in 2009 about 23.5 million people in America suffered from alcohol or illicit drug abuse addictions. Of those, only around 10 percent went to rehab.

Why do so many people who should go, go, go say, "No, no, no"?

We've already talked about denial. A lot of people can't see the severity of their problems, so they don't see the need for help.

We've looked at our problem in four ways, and hopefully we're now past denial and see that we need a path out of our problem.

Another reason people are reluctant to go to rehab is the cost. Rehab centers will often charge $20,000 to $35,000 a month for their treatment programs.

Dang! That is a lot of money!* It's expensive to go to rehab, so a lot of addicts don't go.

But people who say, "I can't afford it!" might not be including the cost of their addictions in their calculations. How much do they spend every month on alcohol or drugs? How much per year? If they continue in their addictions, how much will it cost them over the next decade?

What about the lost career advancement and the negative impact on their physical health? How much does all that cost?

Addiction obviously doesn't carry a purely financial price tag. There are other prices people pay. How many family members are driven away? How many friendships are lost?

My father was a gambling addict. He occasionally came home a winner. When he did, we might buy a Jaguar or jet off to Disney World. Far more often, though, he came home a loser. I can't even imagine how much money he lost over the years.

It also cost him his family. Even his relatives who stuck by him could never trust him.

He burned every friend he ever had.

So how much did his addiction really cost him?

How much is your issue costing you? It's important to count the cost, because you're going to be tempted to quit on this book. This book will force you to look long and hard in the mirror, and that will be uncomfortable. It will ask you to review your past and to be honest about your present. That could be painful.

Reading and really engaging in this book is going to cost you something.

But how much is your issue costing you?

The Bible says you should have peace that passes understanding. Do you?

The Bible says you should have joy. Do you?

---

* Just think, you got this book for less than twenty dollars! So, who's your best friend? That's right, it's me. My birthday is January 29—send me presents!

The Bible says you never need to worry. Do you?

The Bible says you should live a life of freedom. Do you?

The Bible says there is no longer condemnation for you, so you can live a guilt-free life. Do you?

The Bible says you can look at yourself as God's beloved child. Do you?

Think about the future you want for yourself—the relationship you want to have with God, the kind of family you want to have, the impact you'd like to have on this world. If you keep doing what you're doing, will you get to that future? Or are your issues going to keep you from it?

What is your issue costing you? Whatever it is, I'd bet it's more than it would cost you to read and really engage with this book.

Going to Rehab

So, we're going to rehab. Not a rehab *center*, but rehab for the rest of us. Rehab for people with issues that are costing us but that aren't severe enough or socially unacceptable enough to send us to a facility.

If we were actually to go to a rehab facility, there would be some rules we'd have to follow. There aren't rules for reading this book, but I wonder if there might be some ways we should apply some of the common rehab rules.

Rule 1: At rehab, you can't read or watch anything that isn't positive and helpful to your recovery.

Question: What might lead your mind in the wrong direction and distract you from your journey toward healing and wholeness? How could you prevent it from being a negative influence on you?

Rule 2: At rehab, no cell phones or computers are allowed.

Question: To make this journey as powerful as possible, what do you need to go without as you read this book?

Rule 3: At rehab, you would learn that recovery happens in community. There is something empowering about telling your story, having a safe place to share your secrets, realizing that you are not alone, and receiving encouragement and accountability.

Question: How could you read this book and do this journey in community? Perhaps that wasn't your plan, but maybe now you could plan for it. Is there a group you could read this book with? Or is there a friend or two you can call to tell them what you're reading and ask them to join you? You'll be so glad you did.

From No, No, No to Go, Go, Go

All right, enough of looking at our problem. It's time to start walking the path out of our problem. Let's move toward freedom. Are you ready?

It's time for rehab for the rest of us.

STEP 1
I CAN'T; GOD CAN

We are an independent

self-made

pull–yourself–up–by–your–bootstraps

I–don't–need–your–help!

I–got–this

I–can

kind of people.

The only problem is

I can't.

We can't.

But there's good news:

There's someone who can.

More good news:

That someone not only can.

He wants to.

MY PROBLEM WITH ME

ALBERT EINSTEIN HAD a parietal lobe that was 15 percent larger than that of the average brain. So he was pretty smart.

But he also married his cousin.

To be precise, he married a woman who was his first cousin maternally and *also* his second cousin paternally.

That means, if I'm doing my genealogy math correctly, that Albert Einstein's parents were also cousins.

No wonder he had to come up with the theory of relativity! Can you picture the family reunions? Or how about weddings? Relatives must have shown up hours early to study the family tree so they could determine which side to sit on. Maybe they had three sections: Bride's. Groom's. Both.

I, for one, have decided not to give the genius of Albert Einstein such hero status that I emulate all his life decisions. But the crazy-haired dude did have some smart things to say. Three of the smart things he said will help us get into our first step to freedom, which is "I can't; God can."

Insanity

We've admitted we have a problem. In fact, you could even say we're sick. Albert Einstein would say it a different way. He would say we're insane, and I'm not going to disagree with him.*

Einstein is often credited with defining insanity as doing the same thing over and over again but expecting different results.

That makes sense, right?

If I leave home to drive to work, thinking that going south on Las Vegas Boulevard will get me there, only to have it take me farther and farther away from my destination, that was a silly mistake.

If the next day I leave home and go south on Las Vegas Boulevard *again*, the opposite direction from work, that's stupid.

But if I do it again the following day, and the day after that, that's *insane*. There's a craziness going on, and my friends should be concerned.

What if I feel like my life is boring and kind of meaningless, and I try to escape by watching three hours of TV, where I can focus on other people with more interesting lives, and while I'm doing it, my life feels just as boring and meaningless? That's silly. If the next day I come home from work and again escape by watching three hours of TV and again feel empty inside, that's stupid. But if I do it again the following day, and the day after that, that's insane.

Or let's say a person feels bad about herself—the way her life is going, the way she looks—so she drowns her sorrows by eating a tub of ice cream. The next day she's one pound *more* unhappy with herself. Well, that didn't work. But if she does it again? That's getting stupid. Then again, and again? That's insane.

Or you have a guy who, ever since he was little, just wanted respect.

---

* Except maybe about that cousin thing.

When he was preschool age, he would throw temper tantrums if his parents didn't respect him. It didn't work. They never said, "Oh, you just want to be respected? We do respect you, honey." But he just kept throwing temper tantrums. Now he's in his forties, and if his wife or the people at work don't respect him, he lashes out in anger. It *still* doesn't work. No one says, "What you really want is respect. We respect you." But, even still, he keeps doing it. That's insane.

Insanity is doing the same thing over and over again and expecting a different result. When you look at some of the ways we try to find pleasure in life, or try to escape from the pain of life, we're pretty insane.

But we're even crazier than just that. We're also insane in how we try to address our problems.

Have you ever made a decision or a New Year's resolution about your problem?

- "This year I'm going to stop spending so much time on TV and video games and start volunteering more!"
- "I'm going to stop eating so many desserts this year, and I will lose twenty pounds!"
- "I will start counting to ten to calm myself down instead of blowing up at people."
- "I'm going to stop worrying. I just can't do it anymore. No more worrying!"

So you made that decision to stop doing what you do. Did you stop?

I'm going to guess you didn't.[†]

You just kept doing what you said you weren't going to keep doing. Eventually you started to feel bad again, so what did you do? You made the same decision to stop doing what you do.

[†] If you did, I wonder if maybe you didn't stop your problem but rather replaced it with another problem. Maybe you stopped watching so much TV but started spending hours on the Internet. Or maybe you stopped smoking but started overeating. What might have happened is that you traded one unhelpful (maybe even self-destructive) habit for another one.

- "I'm serious this time! I'm going to lose weight!"
- "That's it: I will not look at porn anymore!"
- "I have enough clothes. I will not buy any more for the rest of the year!"

You made the decision to stop doing what you do *again*. Did you stop this time?

I'm going to guess you didn't, *again*.

I will venture that at some point you became frustrated with yourself and . . . you made the same decision to stop *again*. But you didn't stop. *Again*.

Guess what?

You are insane.

I am too.

This leads into the second thing Mr. Smarty-Pants-Who-Married-His-Cousin Albert Einstein said that I think we need to understand to take our first step toward freedom.

Where Do I Find the Solution to My Problem?

It has become very obvious we have a problem. How do we solve our problem? Albert Einstein said, "No problem can be solved from the same level of consciousness that created it."

What does that mean?

There's a reason you do what you do. There's an unmet need it seems to be meeting—perhaps a need for comfort or reassurance or security or validation or control. Or it might be that there's pain it's helping you to ignore—perhaps a deep-seated wound from your childhood or a current hurt from which you want to escape.

There's a reason you do what you do, and you're probably not fully aware of that reason.* You have cauldrons of psychological soup boiling under the surface, and some of the ingredients are a mystery to you.

---

* In counseling or at a rehab center, you might hear about "secondary gains." Basically, a secondary gain is a motivator for addictive behavior that is not the primary reason you do it and that you may not even recognize.

What is the solution I look to for the problems that plague me?
Me.

But *me* is what got me into this trouble in the first place.

I'm guessing you have a me that's a lot like me.

- *Me* is the one who loves to eat entire trays of Oreos. Is *me* really going to convince *me* to stop?
- *Me* is the one who feels important and in the know when I gossip about others. Is *me* really going to get *me* to stop?
- *Me* is the one who, instead of working to improve my marriage, tries to escape it through reading romance novels or through connecting with old friends or strangers online. How in the world is *me* going to change *me*'s behavior?

The solutions we come up with for our problems tend to be of the self-help variety. But the "self" part is the issue. Self is what got me in trouble in the first place. Self is the one who's been doing what I've been doing, and so when I try a self-help solution, I just end up in a war with myself.

So you relying on you—on you being smarter or more disciplined—to get yourself from where you are to where you need to be *isn't* going to work, because you're the one who got yourself where you are. When you're in charge, where you are is where you end up.

I'm not being rude; I'm just being real.

I'm also not judging you. I can't, because I'm just like you. When I look at my problems, I want to point fingers and blame others and play the victim card, but the truth is *I* got myself here. If I'm being honest, *I* can't get myself out. Why? Because "no problem can be solved from the same level of consciousness that created it."

It's not just you and me; *it's all of us.* The apostle Paul is probably the preeminent example of an all-in, disciplined, radical follower of Jesus. Listen to how he describes his life:

I don't really understand myself, for I want to do what is right, but I don't do it. Instead, I do what I hate. But if I know that what I am doing is wrong, this shows that I agree that the law is good. So I am not the one doing wrong; it is sin living in me that does it.

And I know that nothing good lives in me, that is, in my sinful nature. I want to do what is right, but I can't. I want to do what is good, but I don't. I don't want to do what is wrong, but I do it anyway. But if I do what I don't want to do, I am not really the one doing wrong; it is sin living in me that does it.

I have discovered this principle of life—that when I want to do what is right, I inevitably do what is wrong. I love God's law with all my heart. But there is another power within me that is at war with my mind. This power makes me a slave to the sin that is still within me. Oh, what a miserable person I am! Who will free me from this life that is dominated by sin and death?[1]

Permit me to paraphrase that for us:

I don't really understand myself, for I want to do what is right, but I don't do it. I tell myself not to yell at my kids, then I hear someone yelling at my kids, and I realize it's me. There's something wrong inside me that leads me to do what I don't want to do.

I tell myself, "Whatever happens, I will not deviate from my diet. I promise I will not make any exceptions!" Then I find a piece of pizza in my mouth. What a miserable person I am. I am a slave to pizza! As I try to understand this power that makes me a slave to sin, I suddenly have a realization— I am now eating brownies! I am a slave to pizza *and* brownies!

I have discovered this principle of life—that when I want to do right, there's always something wrong for me to look at on the Internet. I don't want to look, but there's something in me that does it anyway.

When I am about to tell my wife that she's just like her mother, I know what I am about to do is wrong. That's why I decide not to tell my wife she's just like her mother. Then I find my mouth opening and words coming out. I hear those words. They sound like . . . "You are just like your mother." It is sin living in me that does that.

Who will free me from this life dominated by the dumb things *me* keeps doing? One thing *me* knows for sure: it's not gonna be *me*!

What am I saying? What was Paul saying? Basically, that no problem can be solved from the same level of consciousness that created it.

That leads into the third thing Einstein said that I think we need to understand to take our first step toward freedom.

Keep Moving

Here's the third quote from Einstein: "Life is like riding a bicycle. To keep your balance you must keep moving."

If you've ever taught a kid to ride a bike, you understand the analogy. The biggest problem new bicyclers have is that when they get nervous, or when they start to feel intimidated by what's approaching, they stop pedaling. The problem is that on a bike, if you're not moving forward, you're falling down.

The problem in life, the problem in taking this journey to freedom, is that if you're not moving forward, you're falling down.

This rehab journey we're on is going to consist of six steps that we'll be taking for the rest of our lives. The first one is "I can't; God can." The beginning of our quest for freedom is recognizing that we have a problem we can't solve. But that epiphany is just the start. We need to keep moving forward. And we will.

But I'm guessing you're not totally convinced that you can't solve your own problem. My *me* is really stubborn that way. Your *me* is probably the same. If we're going to take this all-important "I can't; God can" step to freedom, we have to be *totally* convinced.

You also might be concerned about this idea of always moving forward. If you're like me, you're thinking, *That's part of my problem. Sometimes I just have no momentum, I make no progress, and I* can't *get going in the right direction.*

That's *not* a problem.

In fact, acknowledging that is your salvation.

*   *   *

Hey, if you've been putting it off, maybe you're starting to realize I wasn't joking about not reading this alone. It's not too late to invite someone to read with you! You can also find an online community of fellow readers at TheRestoreCommunity.com. It's totally free to join and will allow you to access more than thirty videos, featuring yours truly, that correspond with the chapters in this book and a free PDF guide to help you stay on track.

THE TOP TEN THINGS I NEED TO CHANGE ABOUT MYSELF

10. Frequent use of the phrase "Va-va-va-voom!"

9. My irrational fear of potatoes.

8. Talking to my popcorn during movies.

7. Prefacing my answer to every question I'm asked by yelling, "Survey says!"

6. Going to the gym to take showers because the body wash is free.

5. Talking to the screen during movies.

4. Trying to have corn dogs spayed or neutered.

3. Constantly referring to myself by my own name, because Vince has a problem with that.

2. Going around to every table at restaurants, licking my lips, and saying, "Mmmmmm, I'd love some of that if it weren't for my infected gums."

1. Eating pancakes in the shower to save time.

DROWNING

WHEN I LIVED IN VIRGINIA BEACH, just off the Atlantic, I would hear about people drowning. In fact, the first ten years I lived there, more than fifty people drowned in the ocean. I knew people drowned fairly frequently; I just never would have guessed that my wife and I would be two of them.

It was late in the summer of 1998, not long after Hurricane Bonnie came ripping through our beachside city. We weren't sufficiently prepared, I think mostly because no one is scared of anything named "Bonnie,"* so there was major damage. It was a long week of being holed up in our house and then helping friends and neighbors with their property damage. A sunny Saturday sprang up and, needing a break, we decided to go to the beach.

---

* The school nurse when I was a kid was named Bonnie, and even if she came at you with a tongue depressor (or a meat cleaver), you just couldn't be afraid of someone named Bonnie.

We arrived and discovered that the city had put up red flags. Red flags mean because the current and waves are rough, they strongly suggest you not go into the ocean. If you do choose to go in, you can't go in deep.

Jen saw the red flags and said, "I guess we'd better not swim."

I laughed. "Yeah, right. C'mon, let's go."*

We walked to the water's edge and realized a bunch of people were in the water—even a group of small kids playing tag—but everyone was staying in shallow water. The kids were up to their knees, the parents up to their ankles. We hung out with the nerds for a while, but standing in ankle-deep water isn't much fun.

I told Jen, "Let's go a little deeper."

Knee deep.

"A little deeper."

Waist deep.

"A little deeper."

Chest deep.

"A little deeper."

Before we knew it, we were in *way* deep. The current was strong and was pulling us out farther. The waves were *huge*. They were the biggest waves we'd ever seen, and one went crashing over our heads.

That's when we realized we could no longer touch bottom.

That's when another wave crashed over our heads.

We came up and tried to catch our breath, but another wave crashed over our heads.

That's when Jen freaked out. She yelled, "I think I'm drowning!"

"No," I stated very logically, "you are not drowning."

My logic didn't work.

"I am!" Jen screamed. "I'm drowning!"

"No"—I was sticking with logic—"you can swim, so just swim in."

---

* Now might be a good time to tell you that, in addition to the other problems I've been sharing with you, I've always struggled with a rebellious personality and a reckless spirit. That's the kind of personality type that helps a person start churches but the kind of personality *disorder* that helps a person get himself, and others, in lots of trouble. Read on for exhibit A.

That's when she screamed the two magic words: "I can't!"

When she said, "I can't," I understood that she was desperate, felt helpless, and wasn't going to even try. She had lost all hope that she could save herself.

Suddenly it hit me: my wife was going to die out here.

I realized if she had any chance, I was going to have to save her.

I should pause here and let you know that I had never taken a lifeguarding class. I had never even seen an episode of *Baywatch*, so I had zero knowledge when it came to water-related lifesaving skills.

But I thought, *How hard can it be? I'll swim over, grab her, and swim to shore.*

I swam over.

I went to grab her.

That's when she grabbed me. She was flailing her arms around, saw that I was close, and decided to climb aboard. She grabbed my head, pushed me underwater, and tried to use me as a flotation device.

That's when I understood that when she said, "I can't," she hadn't *totally* lost all hope that she could save herself. She was still frantically trying to find a way to rescue herself.

I wrestled free from her grip, moved away, caught my breath, and, again, swam over to save her. She, again, grabbed me and thrust me underwater.

That's when it hit me: *We are both going to die out here.*

Saving Yourself

Andrew Delbanco is a humanities professor at Columbia University. Some years back he was attending AA meetings as part of his research on Alcoholics Anonymous. One Saturday morning he found himself in a church basement in New York City. At AA meetings people have a chance to share their stories, and Delbanco listened to a "crisply dressed young man" talk about his problems. The only thing was, they weren't his problems. Everything that was wrong in his life was someone else's fault. Delbanco writes, "Every word and gesture gave the impression of grievously wounded pride." The man believed he hadn't caused his own problems, so he certainly couldn't fix them. He just needed other people to stop victimizing him. While he was speaking, the man sitting next to Delbanco leaned over and whispered to him, "I used to feel that way too, before I achieved low self-esteem."

Delbanco writes,

> This was more than a good line. For me, it was the moment I understood in a new way the religion I had claimed to know something about. As the speaker bombarded us with phrases like "taking control of my life," "believing in myself," "toughing it out," the man beside me took refuge in the old Calvinist doctrine that pride is the enemy of hope. What he meant by his joke about self-esteem was that no one can save himself by dint of his own efforts.[1]

The problem with the guy speaking was that he was drowning, but he still thought he could save himself.

Behavior Modification

The problem when we try to save ourselves is that we just do behavior modification. Self-help is skin deep.

My friend Kyle says it's like a doctor telling a guy with lung cancer to take cough medicine. Yeah, it may get rid of any external signs that there's a problem, but it does nothing to address the root of the problem.

We'd be mortified if a doctor took that approach, yet it's the approach we take to address our own problems all the time. Right?

- If you have a gambling problem, stay away from the casinos.
- If you have an anger problem, take a deep breath and count to ten.
- If your marriage is in trouble, schedule a date night.

- If you're a workaholic, leave the office at five o'clock and don't bring work home.
- If you're in debt, cut up your credit cards.
- If your weight is a problem, go on a diet.

Those might not be bad ideas, but they don't get to the heart of the issue. The heart of the issue is your heart.[2]

Jesus said, "*From the heart* come evil thoughts, murder, adultery, all sexual immorality, theft, lying, and slander."[3]

In Jesus' time, the religious leaders—the Pharisees—were all about being, or at least appearing, right. So their approach was behavior modification. Jesus wasn't exactly impressed. He told them:

What sorrow awaits you teachers of religious law and you Pharisees. Hypocrites! For you are so careful to clean the outside of the cup and the dish, but inside you are filthy—full of greed and self-indulgence! You blind Pharisee! First wash the inside of the cup and the dish, and then the outside will become clean, too. What sorrow awaits you teachers of religious law and you Pharisees. Hypocrites! For you are like whitewashed tombs—beautiful on the outside but filled on the inside with dead people's bones and all sorts of impurity. Outwardly you look like righteous people, but inwardly your hearts are filled with hypocrisy and lawlessness.[4]

I think this helps us understand why religious people today aren't exempt from addictive behavior. It's because Christians today can be way more like the Pharisees than they'd ever care to admit. It seems there's an inherent temptation in religion to make it about being right. Christians want, intellectually, to be right. They want their behavior to be right. At the very least, they want to give the appearance that they're right. But Christianity is *not* about being right; it's about admitting you're wrong—and being so sure you're wrong in your thinking and your behavior that you lose all hope that you can be right and so become desperate for a Savior.

Christianity isn't about being right . . .

- it's about being *real* with God;
- it's about desperately *reaching* out to him;
- it's about feeling him grab you and pull you into *relationship*.

Sister Molly Monahan was a nun with a habit. I speak not of her tunic, but of her addiction to alcohol.*

She had been trained in the practices of Ignatian spirituality, had a graduate degree in theology, and went on annual spiritual retreats, yet she writes, "None of this prevented me from becoming an alcoholic." She couldn't understand why.

I don't know the answer, but I have a guess. My suspicion is that all her religious education trained her to be sure she was right instead of being sure she was wrong.

So what did alcoholic Sister Molly do? She went to a recovery program. She writes in her book *Seeds of Grace* that her recovery program led her into a depth of spirituality and relationship with God like she had never experienced. Why? What was it that her addiction and quest for sobriety taught her that all her religious training had not? She writes, "In my alcoholism I experienced myself as being utterly lost and unable to help (save) myself in a way that I never had before."[5]

In recovery she learned "I can't."

She was drowning, and now she knew she couldn't save herself.

Drowning in the Atlantic

That brings us back to the ocean, where my wife and I were drowning.

I realized† she thought she might still be able to save herself but

---

* I'm sure she also had the tunic, but that's irrelevant for our purposes.
† Through her grabbing me and trying to ride me to shore like a surfboard.

couldn't. So I decided on a sneak-attack strategy. I would slyly get close, reach out as fast as a cobra attacking a rabbit,[‡] grab her, and then swim to shore, pulling her behind me.

I did it. Suddenly I was holding her arm and swimming to shore. I was swimming, against the current, dragging her thrashing body behind me. It wasn't easy. In fact, after a couple of strokes I thought I was going to have a heart attack. So I let go and said, "Jen, try to stand up." She tried but couldn't.

I grabbed her again, swam in a few more strokes, almost *had* a stroke, let go, and again said, "Jen, try to stand up." Again, she tried but couldn't.

So I grabbed her another time, swam in another time, told her to stand another time. She tried another time but still couldn't.

I'm going to be honest. I don't think she tried that time. I'm pretty sure she had given up hope that she'd ever be able to stand. As soon as I let go, before I could even say, "Stand up," she yelled, "I can't!" There wasn't enough time to find out.

That's also what happened the next time and the next time and the time after that.

Finally, I had gotten her in almost all the way, and so I let go and said, "Stand up, Jen." Before the words were out of my mouth, she cried, "I can't!"

But I had gotten her in so far that she was now surrounded by the little children who had been playing tag. They were standing knee deep, circling the floundering lady and shouting, "Stand up! Stand up, lady! It's not hard. You can do it! Look, we can do it. Stand up!"

It was hysterical and it was horrible, all at the same time. Mostly I was flooded with relief because we weren't drowning in the ocean anymore.

It makes me think of the story where Jesus approaches this guy who hasn't been able to walk in thirty-eight years. We get the impression that he's tried everything, but nothing has worked. As he talks,

---

‡ I assume cobras are fast. If not, let's just pretend. And . . . I assume cobras attack rabbits.

it becomes obvious he's drowning in a pool of self-pity. He wants to use his legs, but . . . he can't. Then he meets Jesus. Jesus looks at him and says, "Stand up," and he can. He does. He stands up and walks right into a new life.[6]

You need to know that if you listen for God, you'll hear him saying, "Stand up. You can do it. Well, *you* can't, in your own power. But you can in *mine*."

That's step one into a new life: I can't; God can.

THE POWER I NEED

"Woman Sat on Boyfriend's Toilet for 2 Years."

That was the title of the newspaper article.

Kind of gets your attention.

It seems that in Ness City, Kansas, a thirty-five-year-old woman sat on her boyfriend's toilet . . . for two years! By the time her boyfriend finally called the police for help, her body was stuck to the seat. The Ness County sheriff explained, "She was not glued. She was not tied. She was just physically stuck by her body." He said it appeared her skin had grown around the seat.[1]

Each day her boyfriend had brought her food and water and asked her to come out of the bathroom. Her reply? "Maybe tomorrow."

Finally, on February 27, 2008, the boyfriend decided that two years on the toilet was enough.

Police reported that the clothed woman was sitting on the toilet, her sweat pants down to her mid-thigh, that she was "somewhat disoriented," and her legs looked like they had atrophied.

A neighbor, upon hearing of the situation, said, "It really doesn't surprise me."

What kind of neighborhood do these people live in?!

When I first read this story, I didn't know how to respond. I read it again, thinking, *There is no way this can be true*, and asking myself questions like, *But how? Why? Why did the boyfriend wait two years? Why didn't the woman just get up?*

Then I realized—I am that woman.

I've never sat on a toilet for two years,* but looking back at times in my life when I felt stuck, I can't believe I stayed in the situation for so long. I can clearly recall that feeling of helplessness. I remember moments when I knew what I had to do to get unstuck, but I would just say, "Maybe tomorrow."

I think we've all done time on the toilet.

In fact, there's probably some area of your life where you feel stuck right now.

It might be your relationship with your parents. You've been stuck in the same unhealthy patterns with them for years.

Or you have a job you hate, but it seems there are no other options.

It could be you look at things on the Internet that make you feel good for a minute then guilty for hours. You've sworn a thousand times that it would never happen again, but it always happens again. You are stuck.

Maybe you're overweight or have high cholesterol or high blood pressure and you've committed to making changes, but you didn't stay committed to your commitment, and change has not come.

Or you might feel stuck spiritually. There's something holding you back from taking the next steps in your faith journey.

You might say it's worse. Your situation goes beyond being stuck; a better word to describe it is *dead*.

---

* Though my wife might beg to differ.

Maybe your marriage feels dead. Constant fighting has drained all the passion out of it, and now it feels utterly lifeless.

Or it could be your finances. You've buried yourself under debilitating debt and there seems to be no way out.

How do you get unstuck? How do you get un*dead*?

Stuck

At twenty years old, I had never been to church, didn't think I had ever known a Christian, and started reading the Bible for the first time. I couldn't relate to most of the people I read about.

I had never built an ark like Noah.

I had never stolen my brother's birthright like Jacob.

I had never made a golden calf like Aaron or burned one like Moses.

I *had* danced in my underwear like David, but that seemed like a periphery part of his story, and I had definitely never killed a giant with a sling.

But there was one guy I could relate to. His name was Peter, and he seemed like maybe the biggest idiot in the whole book. That's why I kind of identified with him. The more I read about this guy, the more I realized he was stuck in the same old, same old.

Peter was a fisherman, and every day he would get up and . . . go fishing. The next day was more fishing, and the day after that was more fishing. Nothing ever changed. I bet Peter wondered, *Is this all there is to life? Doesn't there have to be more than this?*

Then one day Jesus invited Peter to follow him around and learn a new way of living. Peter gave up the whole fishing biz and started learning from Jesus. Because he always seemed to be with Jesus, we get to see a lot of him in the Bible, and we learn he was stuck in all kinds of ways.

He was stuck with some serious personality flaws. He had a big mouth. He would talk before he thought and say things he would later regret. He also had anger issues—like the time he attacked some dude with a sword.

Peter was also stuck in fear. One time when Peter was in a boat, Jesus came walking out to the boat on the water. Peter—who, remember, always said things before he thought them out—said, "Can I walk on water to you?" Jesus smiled* and said, "Get to steppin', brother."† So Peter got out of the boat, put his feet on the water, and started walking to Jesus. He was staring right at Jesus the whole time, and he was actually walking on water. Then he noticed the waves were high and the winds strong, and he looked around, and he began sinking. He screamed in fear, and the whole thing went from super cool to super embarrassing.[2]

Then there was the time Jesus got arrested and put on trial for claiming to be the Son of God. What Jesus needed was a friend, someone to stand with him. That's when someone went up to Peter and asked, "Hey, aren't you one of Jesus' friends?" Peter said no. Three times he was asked if he was a friend of Jesus, and three times he denied it. One time he even swore and cursed to make his denial more convincing.[3] Why? He was stuck in fear.

The next morning, Jesus was crucified. I think that day Peter went from feeling stuck to feeling dead. He must have felt dead spiritually. He had never been a spiritual giant, but he *had* gotten to be with Jesus for three years. He had learned a lot. He had grown in his faith and hope for the future. But now he wouldn't get to be with Jesus anymore. Jesus was dead, and so was Peter's faith and hope.

Then Jesus rose from the dead.‡

Peter learned that Jesus' supernatural power was greater than stuckness. It was greater than *death*.

So Peter got unstuck. His life went from same old, same old to

---

* Well, the Bible doesn't say Jesus smiled. I'm kind of assuming that.

† Well, the Bible doesn't say Jesus said, "Get to steppin', brother." I'm paraphrasing.

‡ If you're reading this and you're not someone who believes in Jesus, it might surprise you to know that there are volumes of evidence supporting the fact that Jesus actually rose from the dead. In fact, back when I was twenty, I went from a cynic to a believer through studying the evidence for the Resurrection.

an unbelievable adventure. He went from having a fickle, bombastic personality to being solid as a rock. He was no longer a prisoner of fear. In fact, we see him through the rest of the Bible standing up to incredible intimidation. Later he was willing to die for Jesus.

Peter got unstuck. But how?

It wasn't through his own power. Peter had become very familiar with "I can't." He had tried on his own, and he always failed. It was only when he gave up and relied on God's power that he finally got unstuck and found new life. He later said as much when he wrote, "By his divine power, God has given us everything we need for living a godly life."[4]

I wonder if Peter, later in his life, now unstuck, thought back on that day when he walked on water and realized, *When I looked into Jesus' eyes, when I made it about Jesus, I could walk on water. But when I looked away, when it became about me and what I was up against, that's when I got stuck. The secret all along was Jesus. I had to find a power greater than myself. I couldn't get myself unstuck, but Jesus could.*

Isn't that just like us? When we focus on the power of our problems and whether we can get past them, we get stuck. Peter did the impossible only when he looked not at his problem or to his own ability but at Jesus and his impossible-defying power.

Give Up or Look Up

The good news for stuck people like you and me is that we have that same power available to us.[§] We've all tried to get unstuck. When it doesn't work, we reach a point where we feel like giving up. That's an option, but not one that ever helped anyone. There's another option: to look up.

You admit you can't, but trust that God can. You start to view God as your "refuge and strength, an ever-present help in trouble."[5] You cry out to him for help, not as a one-time thing but as a pattern that predominates your life. You replace your self-destructive addiction

---

§ See, for instance, Romans 8:11.

with an addiction to self-humbling. You become daily dependent on God's power.

Why *wouldn't* we do that? Why wouldn't we cry out to God for help?

Some of us don't accurately understand our condition. Others of us may not feel our situation is desperate enough. Or it may be we believe our personal resources to handle it are sufficient.

I was talking to the director of a rehab center the other day. She said to me, "I know the Bible says the Israelites were God's chosen people, but personally, I believe addicts are God's chosen people." I liked the sound of that, so I asked her to explain. She said, "Addicts feel desperate, so they cry out for help. Normal people feel desperate, so they watch TV."

She's right. You can be desperate and *not* cry out for help.

We may not cry out for help because we don't like to feel desperate. So we numb ourselves, maybe by watching TV or by playing games on our phones or by flipping through Instagram or by drinking a couple of glasses of wine. We sit there, stuck, and we say, "Maybe tomorrow."

We may not cry out for help because we don't like to feel dependent. We like to think of ourselves as independent, autonomous, pull-ourselves-up-by-our-bootstraps individuals. But asking for help is *not* a sign of weakness; it's a sign of *strength*. Cowards are afraid to ask for help. It takes real courage to admit we can't do it on our own and need a power we don't possess.

The power we need *is* a power we don't possess. To get unstuck we're going to have to access God's power. And if you feel dead, lucky for you his power has proved greater than the grave.

We need to look up and ask for God's power. Because God's power is what stuck people—and dead people—really need.

New Life

Our band finished the opening song, and I walked onstage to welcome the sparse crowd to the service for the fifth week of our new church.

"Welcome to Verve!" (When the crowd is light, you have to *create* the energy.) "My name is Vince, and I'm glad you're here. Today we're going to talk about being spiritually dead."

Little did I know that Warren was in the audience. Actually, I didn't know Warren at all. This was his first time at our church. He had come to destroy it.

By profession, Warren was an evil fire-breathing clown in a horror show in Las Vegas. By philosophy, Warren was a hardcore, angry atheist. Warren had heard there was a new church starting in his city and decided to do something about it. He realized a brand-new church wouldn't have many people and that the people showing up would not be very committed. He decided to go to one of the church's first services, sit in the center of the room, and wait. And in the middle of the service, when the pastor walked onstage to give the sermon, Warren would stand up and let loose a barrage of profanity and throw some chairs, maybe even fists. He figured the people, still making up their minds about the church, would never come back. The church wouldn't be able to survive without people, and Warren could brag for the rest of his life that he had killed a church.

"Today we're going to talk about being spiritually dead," I said. "Perhaps you're spiritually dead but don't know it. That makes me wonder: Can you be *physically* dead and not know it? Just in case, I thought I'd share with you the top ten signs you are physically dead." They were stupid. Like, "You haven't breathed in over twenty-four hours" and "You keep hearing organ music and people saying, 'He looks so natural.'"

Little did I know that Warren was laughing.

The sermon was out of the biblical book of Ephesians. In Ephesians we learn bad news: "As for you, you were dead in your transgressions and sins."[6] God is telling us we don't just *feel* stuck; we *are* stuck. And it's worse than stuck. We are dead.

Have you noticed dead people don't have a lot of power? They usually can't run fast or lift much weight. Dead people are powerless, and we are powerless over our problems.

Little did I know that Warren felt dead.

But the sermon also shared good news from Ephesians: "I also pray that you will understand the incredible greatness of God's power for us who believe him. This is the same mighty power that raised Christ from the dead."[7]

The same power God used to raise Jesus from the dead is available to us. If you feel dead in some area of your life, you don't need to stay dead, because resurrection power is available to you. If you feel stuck, you don't need to stay stuck, because if God can get Jesus unstuck from death in a grave, he can certainly get you unstuck from whatever situation you find yourself in.

The service ended, and Warren realized he hadn't disrupted it. He had become so engaged in the service, he forgot he had come to ruin it.

Warren was sufficiently intrigued to come back the following week, and then the week after that. Soon he was coming to *all three* of our identical services. I asked him why, and this fire-breathing, hardcore atheist said, "I just . . . I just can't get enough of Jesus."

Next Warren took our Verge course. It's a six-week class for people who don't believe but are perhaps on the verge of faith. In Verge, Warren heard about the God who loved him so much he sent Jesus for him. He learned about the volumes of evidence that prove the veracity of the Bible and especially that Jesus' resurrection actually happened. Warren listened to God's offer of relationship through faith in Jesus. Soon Warren learned how to plug into God's power on a daily basis.*

Warren made the decision to put his faith in Jesus.

I don't know if his faith was perfect, but I do know it didn't have to be. Because it's not the *amount* of faith but the *object* of faith that matters.

You may find that encouraging. Perhaps you worry that your faith isn't strong enough, or you feel bad because you have doubts mixed

---

* We'll be learning that in this book as well.

in with your faith. That's okay. It's the object of your faith, not the amount of faith that matters.

That's *always* true.

My hometown—Hammondsport, New York—is on Keuka Lake. In the winter the lake freezes. Let's say two of us are standing in front of this frozen lake. One of us is full of faith: "The lake is frozen and the ice is thick. It will support us! Peter walked on water; we shall walk on ice!" The other one has a little faith but also a lot of doubt: "I'm not sure. It does seem to be frozen, but the ice looks too thin to hold us." If we both make the decision to venture out on the ice, it doesn't matter how much faith one of us has or how little the other has. We will both be held up by the ice, or we will both fall through the ice. It will not matter the *amount* of our faith but the *object* of our faith. If the ice is worthy of our trust, it will hold us. If it's not, it will not.

It's all about—and always about—the object of your faith. Who or what you put your faith in is the critical piece. So I have to say: I understand the strategy the twelve-step community uses of making the "Higher Power" vague so as not to exclude anyone. I love their desire to offer a path of healing to as many people as possible. But what higher power you choose makes all the difference. Seeking a generic god may be a good starting place, but ultimately there's only one Higher Power who overcame the grave and can give you the resurrection power you need.

That's the higher power Warren chose.

Soon he was standing in our parking lot by the Dumpster, about to get baptized in a kiddie pool.[†] I love the imagery of baptism. A person is lowered underwater, which represents being lowered into a grave. Then the person is raised out of the water, which represents resurrection. The believer is coming out of the water to live a new life, not in his or her own power, but in God's.

I handed Warren a microphone so he could share his story with the couple dozen people there to watch. He said, "I have a confession to make! I didn't come here for this. I came here because I hated

---

[†] We roll classy in Las Vegas!

you! I hated every single one of you, and I knew I was stronger than you! But something has happened to me here. I've learned that God loves me. I don't understand that, because I'm a broken man. And I'm an addict. But God loves me, and I just want more of God's love. And . . ." Warren couldn't continue, because what had started as a few sniffles and tears erupted into full-body sobs. He couldn't control himself. He handed the mic back, and we lowered him into the water.

Warren came out of the water undead and with the power he needed to become unstuck.

That same power is available to you and me.

We just need to look up and say, "Help."

The best day to do it is not "maybe tomorrow."

It's today.

THE TOP TEN THINGS I CAN'T DO ON MY OWN

10. Play tug-of-war.

9. Have a child.

8. Sing karaoke to Sonny & Cher's "I Got You Babe."

7. Set the timer on my VCR.

6. Figure out why I still have a VCR.

5. Play Ping-Pong.

4. Eat the "2 for $20" meal at Applebee's.

3. Perform synchronized swimming.

2. Ride a tandem bike.

1. Cuddle.

CLINGING TO GOD'S LOVE

HE WAS A GRIZZLY OLD GUY. Think Jack Palance.* I first saw him two minutes earlier, he was now taking me away in his pickup truck, and I didn't know how to feel about that.

I was speaking at a leadership retreat in South Dakota. There was a free afternoon, and one of the guys asked if I'd like to go snowmobiling with his pastor. I said sure. His pastor was the Jack Palance guy. Before we left, he announced to the group, "You'll know we're back when you see the whites of our eyes." I didn't know what that meant. I wasn't sure I wanted to know.

In his truck I thanked him, and he told me that he loved to take people snowmobiling. In fact, he had just gotten back two days earlier from a snowmobiling trip with his son and a couple of friends. His

---

* If you don't know who Jack Palance is, use a thing called the Internet to look him up. Or just think of a tough old cowboy with leather for skin whose voice sounds like he's had large deposits of gravel in his throat for years.

wife, who was in the truck with us, asked, "What time did you get back that night?" He grumbled, "I don't know. A couple o'clock."

He started telling me his story. He had grown up on a farm in Nebraska. Then Uncle Sam came calling, and he joined the military for a couple of years, including one very rough year in Vietnam. He came home a raging alcoholic.

Same Old, Same Old

Peter grew up on the shores of the Sea of Galilee. He became a fisherman on those waters. Then Jesus came calling, and Peter joined his followers for a couple of years.

Now that he was a follower of Jesus, Peter thought his life was changed forever. He was becoming a leader in a revolution of love that would change the world! His life was an unpredictable, unending, and unstoppable adventure!

Then Jesus died, and it all stopped. Not only did Jesus die, but Peter had a total blowout when he denied Jesus three times at his friend's greatest moment of need. Peter proved himself weak and a failure, and he thought he was disqualified from ever serving God again.

So Peter went back to fishing. Right back to the same old, same old.

When Pastor Jack Palance came back from the war, his "same old" became drinking till the bottle was empty. Barroom fights and arrests and spending nights in jail also became part of his new, postwar normal.

Perfect Love for Imperfect People

Peter went back to his old life of fishing. Then Jesus rose from the dead. Peter learned Jesus had resurrection power. That was the power Peter needed, because the power he needed was a power he didn't possess.

But it turns out he needed something else, too. That's why he was *still* stuck. That's why, even *after* the Resurrection, we find him back out fishing on the Sea of Galilee with his buddies. That's when one of them recognized that the guy standing over on the beach was Jesus.

Then, "when Simon Peter heard that it was the Lord, he put on his tunic (for he had stripped for work), jumped into the water, and headed to shore."[1]

Peter had stripped like a Chippendales dancer to go *fishing* and then put clothes *on* to go *swimming*.* He was in a hurry to get to Jesus, but he also had to be very nervous. Remember, very recently, Peter had denied three times that he even knew Jesus. No one stood up for Jesus, and he was crucified. So what would Jesus do with Peter and his sin?

What Jesus did was let Peter know his sin wasn't too big to forgive. Jesus showed Peter that Jesus still had a place in his heart for him and a place of leadership for him in his church. That's when Peter discovered there is something stronger than even resurrection power: the unmitigated, irrepressible force of God's unconditional love.

That love rebuilt, redeemed, and repaired Peter's broken life. Jesus loved Peter with a love that restored worth, dignity, and value to Peter. After this encounter, Peter became a bold leader in the church, one who ended up willing to die for Jesus. That bold Peter never would have existed if it weren't for the unbelievable, life-transforming force of God's unconditional love.

Peter couldn't tap into God's power when he felt like he was too sinful to approach God. But on the beach that day he learned that God is not just powerful; he is compassionate. Being loved with God's perfect love, when Peter was anything but perfect, changed him forever.

The same is true for you and me. If we don't understand God's compassion, we won't go to him for the resurrection power that can give us new life.

But it's not just that God's love invites us to access his power, which we need in order to be transformed; it's that God's love is what we need to be transformed. God's love changes the direction of our lives.

---

* Picture a confused look on my face.

But

When I was young, my English teachers taught me not to start sentences with the word *but*. But I didn't agree. Sometimes you have to start a sentence with "but" to signify that there's been a complete change of direction from what came before the "but."

Check this out: remember that sermon Warren heard from Ephesians, where the Bible says, "As for you, you were dead in your transgressions and sins"?[2] The next couple of verses paint an even bleaker picture of our condition. It's bad.

But then there's this sentence that starts with the word *but*:

> But God is so rich in mercy, and he loved us so much, that even though we were dead because of our sins, he gave us life when he raised Christ from the dead. (It is only by God's grace that you have been saved!)[3]

My English teachers were fools, because that is one of the greatest sentences I've ever read. There are multiple Bible passages that describe how we've messed up and gotten stuck, followed by an amazing sentence starting with that amazing word, *but*, signifying a complete change of direction. I'm just saying: thank God for the but!

Maybe you've never been thankful for God's but, but you should be. Because when God puts his but into our situation, it changes everything. I actually have this idea of making a line of Christian T-shirts with sayings like:

- Saved . . . by God's But
- I Once Was Lost, until My Encounter with God's But
- God So Loved the World, He Gave Us His But
- Get Off Your Butt and Grab God's But
- God's Amazing But, How Sweet the Sound!

These T-shirts will either make me a millionaire or get me burned at the stake.

Speaking of being burned at the stake, I probably have a bunch of English teachers who are mad at me, so I'm going to win back their love with a little grammar lesson.

That passage in Ephesians ended with "It is only by God's grace that you have been saved."

Grace means to get the opposite of what you deserve. God loves us despite us, not because of us. He loves us not because of what we do, but because of who he is. When we're at our worst, God's love is at its best.

That verse says that because of grace—God's unconditional love—you have been *saved*. That word *saved* is written in the perfect tense. My old English teachers would tell you a verb can be one of several tenses, like past, present, future, or perfect tense.

- Past tense is speaking about something that has already happened.
- Present tense is describing something happening right now.
- Future tense is talking about something that will happen eventually but hasn't yet.
- Present perfect tense refers to something that has happened in the past, is still happening in the present, and will continue in the future. It draws attention to the continuing effects of something that has happened in the past.

And "saved" is written in present perfect tense! It means you were saved by God's grace in the past, but the effect of that will *always* continue in your life. That means God will continue giving you new life in your dead places until his work in you is complete. That means you *never* have to feel defeated, and you can never give up. It means God didn't just save you; he *saves* you.

You can't, but God can, and God *will*, if you turn to his power and his love.

Back on day 2 I told you about Heather Kopp. She was stuck for years but finally moved past her addiction to alcohol. How? Did she gain self-control and find the inner strength to say no to booze? No. It was just the opposite. She finally realized she *lacked* self-control and strength, and the source of her healing and victory would have to come from outside herself. She writes, "If I was ever going to experience the kind of ongoing spiritual transformation I so desperately wanted, I would have to learn the difference between ascribing to a set of Christian beliefs that had no power to change me, and clinging daily to an experience of God's love and grace that could."[4]

It was God's but that changed her direction. God saved her. Not once but every single day as she clung to his love.

Snowmobiling Theology

The same thing happened to snowmobiling Jack Palance.

He went to a wedding, where he got drunk. Nothing unusual there. *But* at the wedding he met a lady.

Not long afterward, he was arrested for causing trouble in a drunken stupor. Same old, same old. *But* at trial, the judge ordered him to attend AA meetings. Against his will, he started attending. To his surprise, the meetings had an effect.

Meanwhile, the lady he met at the wedding was invited to a tent revival. She went and met Jesus for the first time.

She and Jack Palance had stayed in touch after the wedding, and they went out one night, and she told him the name of the Higher Power he was learning about and starting to look to for sobriety. His name was Jesus. Jack gave his life to Jesus, and everything changed. Like "start the next sentence with a *but*" changed. He was stuck in a daily dependence on alcohol but overcame it with a daily dependence on God's love.

He was so appreciative of God's gift of grace in Jesus that he *had* to share it with others. So he went off to Bible college and became a pastor. He now ministers to farmers and Native Americans in the Middle of Nowhere, South Dakota.

That story took most of our drive.

Finally we arrived and started snowmobiling.

It was fun, but I was nervous. Not for my own safety but for his snowmobile, as I had never driven one. At one point he stopped to tell me we were about to go off the path a little and not to be afraid. I told him my only fear was of breaking his snowmobile. He growled, "Can I ask you something?" I wasn't going to say no to Jack Palance, so I nodded. He said, "I believe God gives his children good gifts. Do you believe that?"

"Yes."

"And God honors those who honor him?"

"Sure."

"So," he continued, "you have devoted your life to serving God, and today he has given you the gift of this snowmobile to use. Do you really think God would allow you to hurt that snowmobile when he's given it to you as a gift?" Before I could answer, he snarled, "There is *no* way he would allow you to hurt that snowmobile when he's given it to you as a gift."

"I guess so," I said, agreeing mostly because I was afraid of him.

"I guess so!" Jack sounded a little upset. "There is *no* way God would allow you to hurt that snowmobile when he's given it to you as a gift!"

Then I pointed at the snowmobile his wife was sitting on, which was missing most of its front section and was held together by duct tape. "What happened to that one?" I asked.

"Oh," he answered, "I took a missionary out snowmobiling, and he ran it into a tree."

He didn't seem to see the irony. I tried not to laugh.

We sped away, and I thought about how I liked his theology, and I wished I could have it, but I just can't. The reality is that God has given us free will, and that means we *can* mess up the good gifts he's given us. God had given this guy the gift of life, but he had messed it up all those years with his alcoholism.

Soon he stopped again. I figured it was for another theology lesson, but this time it was about snowmobiling. He told me, "We're gonna get into more dangerous situations now. So far you've found it easy to keep moving in the right direction. But as we go off the path, the surface below you will be more uneven, and you may start to fall. When you do, lean in the *opposite* direction and *pick up speed*. The most natural thing will be to lean in the direction of the fall and lay off the gas, but go against your instinct and do the opposite."

We drove away and I thought, *Wow*. That's *probably what changed his life*. It *was* a theology lesson. The reality is when we find ourselves starting to fall into sin, the most natural thing is to *stop* moving toward God and let ourselves fall. It's easy: the temptation is there, and it feels like God *isn't*. Unfortunately, any thoughts we do have of God can be filled with shame: "What must he think of me in this moment, as I'm tempted and starting to fall into this temptation?"

The answer to that question is grace. God loves us despite us, not because of us. He loves us not because of what we do but because of who he is. Grace means we can't lose God's love. When we're at our worst, God's love is at its best.

So instead of shrinking away from God in shame and falling into sin, we turn away from the sin and we fall into God. In that moment grace becomes not an idea we understand or a concept we believe in, but something we experience and desperately rely on.

We cling to God's love.

His *but* becomes our reality as our direction is changed and we are overwhelmed with the liberating truth: I can't; God can.

GOD? OR THE STICK?

It's THE MOST famous stick in the Bible. To be fair, it may be the *only* stick in the Bible.

You might think you'd never be tempted to worship a stick, or to put your hope in a stick, but, well, you may have been tempted with this one. If you did worship it or put your hope in it, it would be a problem.

In fact, that may actually be your problem. Because you have a stick of your own, and it may be what you worship and put your hope in. It could be a stick God gave you and is using in your life, but it's still just a stick.

Dude, It's the Stick!

Moses had grown up in the palace, but after he murdered an Egyptian, he became a fugitive shepherd* and stuttered like Porky Pig. You

---

* I would like to create a TV show called *The Fugitive Shepherd*. The main character would always be one step ahead of the law and one step behind his flock of sheep. Sometimes the cops would come close to capturing him, but at the last moment he'd always be able to pull the wool over their eyes. Okay, I'd better stop.

wouldn't guess he'd be God's first choice to speak for him and to demand that Pharaoh free God's people from slavery, but you'd be wrong.

Moses didn't think he was the right choice either. He was also wrong. God asked; Moses objected, repeatedly. Finally, God posed a different question to Moses: "What's in your hand?" I wonder what Moses thought. *Does God not recognize a stick when he sees one? Why is he even asking? This doesn't seem pertinent to our discussion.* Moses answered, "It's a stick."

God then told Moses he would use the stick to prove Moses was, indeed, speaking for God. The stick would become a snake and would do miracles.

That's exactly what happened. Moses used the stick like a magic wand to authenticate his claim that he was God's spokesperson.

The stick became a snake.

The stick was used to perform miracles. Lots of them.

When the Israelites had the Egyptian armies behind them and the Red Sea in front of them, it looked like all was lost. Then Moses had an epiphany. *Wait, I've got that stick!* He held the stick over the water, and the Red Sea parted.

Later the Israelites were stuck in the desert, thirsty and dehydrated. They didn't know what to do, but God said, "The stick, Moses. Use the stick!" So Mo hit a rock with the stick a few times, and water burst out of it like the Bellagio Fountains.[1]

I assume that stick became legendary. It had to!

Moses would be walking past, and people would say, "Look, it's the stick! Oh, and Moses."

People were getting tattoos of the stick.

Someone started a "NotTheStick" Twitter account.

Paparazzi followed the stick to try and get pictures of it with Kanye or Bieber.

People started telling jokes highlighting the stick's growing, almost mythological status:

- When the boogeyman goes to sleep at night, he checks his closet for the stick.
- The stick can light a fire by rubbing two ice cubes together.
- Some people wear Superman pajamas. Superman wears the stick pajamas.
- The stick doesn't mow his lawn. He stands on his porch and dares it to grow.

Then it happened. It actually happened right after Moses hit the rock with the stick. What happened is the Amalekites attacked the Israelites.[2] The Israelites were God's people; the Amalekites were the thorn in the side of God's people. It seemed like every time they turned around, the Amalekites were attacking again.

Maybe you can relate to that, because I've noticed I'm not very creative when it comes to my hang-ups and bad habits. I haven't woken up one day and found myself struggling with bitterness against Lady Gaga or Gandhi or Captain Kangaroo. No, my struggle with bitterness has always been toward my dad. I've never woken up with an urge to get some chewing tobacco or to start hoarding. No, the things that tempt me have been tempting me for a long time. I've been battling my signature sins for years. We all know what it's like to have ongoing battles with the ongoing thorns in our flesh. We've all got our Amalekites.

So the Amalekites attacked, and things looked desperate for the Israelites. They didn't know what to do. Then it hit Moses—the stick! He told his guys to go fight the next day, and he would hold up the stick. He believed that holding up the stick would give the Israelites victory in their battle.

So the Israelites ran toward the battle, and Moses raised the stick like John Cusack holding up his boom box in *Say Anything . . . .*

I don't know for sure, but I have a guess what Moses was expecting. All the other miracles God had done through him and the stick happened *instantly*, so I'll bet Moses thought they would win the battle immediately. The Israelites would charge the front lines and the Amalekites would just fall dead or run away. That's not what happened. The battle went on for quite a while. Spoiler alert: God *did* give the Israelites victory, but it was a Crock-Pot miracle, not a microwave miracle. Why didn't God just end the battle immediately? Why did the Israelites have to fight? I don't know, but he must have had his reasons.

Moses held up the stick, and the Israelites were defeating the Amalekites. Yes! But then Moses' arms got tired, so he put the stick down, and the Amalekites were defeating the Israelites. No! Up, down, winning, losing. Finally, Moses, feeling exhausted and desperate, got some of his buds to hold up his arms. With the stick permanently up in the air, the Israelites defeated the Amalekites.

To commemorate the victory, Moses built an altar and called it "The LORD is my banner."[3] What did Moses mean by "banner"? I did a little research. Turns out in ancient times a banner was usually a flag or a pole with a shiny ornament on top. It was used to show the soldiers the rallying point in a battle.

Did you notice what Moses' banner was? He said, "The LORD is my banner." I might have expected, "The *stick* is my banner," because that stick had some serious awesome sauce. It would have been very tempting for everyone to worship and put their hope in the stick. But it was clear to Moses that the stick was just a tool God chose to use. I'm sure Moses was an appreciative fan of the stick, but he gave all the credit to God.

Your Stick?

You have a stick. Right? There's something you've looked to for help to get you past your problem.

Your stick might be your own determination and strength or your church or your pastor or your twelve-step group or your spouse or your counselor or your Weight Watchers group or a friend.

There's nothing wrong with using a stick. God was the one who decided to have Moses use a stick. If you have a stick that's helping you, keep using it. But don't get confused. It's just a stick—a stick that God is choosing to use in your life, but still, just a stick.

You can't. God can.

Your stick can't. But God can use it.

God is the one who provides the power and love we need to get past our past and move into a better future.

I just have to wonder: Is it possible you've been looking to a stick, or maybe a series of sticks, and have never *truly* looked to God for the healing and strength you need? Perhaps you've given "trusting God" some lip service, but you've really been putting your hope in something else.

We can't; God can.

Prepare My Horse?

What would it look like for you to make the Lord your banner? Practically speaking, how would you put your trust in God as the only one who can, but at the same time use whatever stick he's provided you?

I'm not the biggest fan of quotes about horses, but there's a great one in the Bible that I think can help us: "The horse is prepared for the day of battle, but the victory belongs to the LORD."[4]

That verse is talking about a literal battle, like the one the Israelites fought against the Amalekites. It perfectly describes what the Israelites did that day.

They trusted God for the victory. That's why Moses was on the sidelines, arms heavy, holding up the stick. The Israelites knew they were toast without God, and it was only through his power that they would defeat the Amalekites. If there was going to be victory, it would belong to the Lord.

But here's what they *didn't* do: they didn't just stand there, watching and waiting to see how God was going to defeat the Amalekites. No, they prepared their horses for battle. They sharpened their swords.

They put on their helmets and bulletproof vests.* Then they went into battle. If you watched them in battle, they wouldn't have looked any different from any other army. They were riding their horses and swinging their swords and throwing their grenades.† They wouldn't have looked different from any other army, but there was something *completely* different from every other army—the Lord was their banner. That's why crazy Moses was over there holding up the crazy stick. Though they prepared their horses for battle,‡ they believed victory belonged to the Lord.

When you decide "I can't; God can," you become a "prepare your horse for battle, but victory belongs to the LORD" kind of person. That means you trust that God can and will give you victory. That *doesn't* mean you just sit around, eating chips and guacamole, watching to see how God is going to do it. No, you do what you need to do, but while you do it, you rely completely on God. You're praying it's a stick he'll choose to use in your deliverance. Your attention is on God, and even if you grow weary, even if you have to get some of your buds to help you, you keep it fixed on God.

So, like the Israelites, you might not look different from any other person fighting a similar battle. Just like them, you show up for your counseling session or to your support group meeting, or you read the book someone suggested, or you install the filtering software on your computer, or you start getting up early to exercise, or you create a budget. But *unlike* them, before you do it, while you do it, and after you do it, you *pray*. I'm not talking courtesy prayers; I'm talking constant, *desperate* prayers.

Before you read the book your friend suggested: *God, let me get some wisdom from this. If there's something that can help me in here, point it out and use it in my life.*

While you're listening to your counselor or friend or support group leader, you have an undercurrent of prayer: *God, this person is*

---

* I'm beginning to realize I know nothing about ancient war attire.
† Now realizing I know nothing about ancient weapons of war.
‡ And loaded up their lasers?

great, but . . . a great stick. *Only you can make this really work in my life. Please use this.*

After you create the budget: *God, this budget makes sense, and if I use it, I will stop overspending and eventually get out of debt. But I know I can't live out this budget on my own. I'll end up buying something I can't afford like I have in the past. This has to be you, God. Please empower me to live by this. I can't do this, God, but you can.*

What do you do? You prepare the horse for battle, but you know victory belongs to the Lord. You make God your banner.

My Friend Mike

That's what helped my friend Mike.

Mike's wife attended our church, and Mike came with her occasionally, always reeking of alcohol. He was a drink-every-day, fall-down drunk. Finally his wife, after suffering years of alcohol-induced disappointment and abuse, kicked him out. She didn't want a divorce; she wanted him to change. So . . . he moved in with and started sleeping with another woman.

But somehow, in the middle of this ugly chapter of his life, he turned to Jesus. He started pursuing Jesus with the same intensity he had pursued alcohol. He stopped drinking. He was repeatedly tempted, but every time he turned in desperation to God, and every time God gave him victory.

Mike used to wait for the temptations to finally come to an end, assuming God would take them away. God didn't. Mike's was a Crock-Pot, not a microwave, miracle. He continued to be tempted. But he began to see it as a good thing, because every time he was tempted, he had to move in close to God.

Back when Mike was living with the other woman, she, oddly, bought him a Bible. It was that Bible that led him to start pursuing and eventually turn to Jesus. In the midst of his drunkenness and adultery, he read of God and his unconditional love. Later, after he had put his faith in Jesus, reunited with his wife, and came back to our church, he gave me the Bible. He felt it was wrong to have it because of who gave it to him, but he didn't want to throw out a Bible.

As I looked through the Bible, I noticed that Mike had scribbled a note to himself in the back cover. It said, "Psalm 91." I turned and read it. Psalm 91 begins:

> *Whoever dwells in the shelter of the Most High*
> *   will rest in the shadow of the Almighty.*
> *I will say of the LORD, "He is my refuge and my fortress,*
> *   my God, in whom I trust."*[5]

It ends:

> *"Because he loves me," says the LORD, "I will rescue him;*
> *   I will protect him, for he acknowledges my name.*
> *He will call on me, and I will answer him;*
> *   I will be with him in trouble,*
> *   I will deliver him and honor him.*
> *With long life I will satisfy him*
> *   and show him my salvation."*[6]

I think that's what gave Mike victory over his addiction. The Lord was his banner.

BECAUSE I'M GOD'S CHILD, I GIVE MY LIFE TO HIS WILL

Once we realize we can't but God can,

we're faced with a decision.

Will we keep on trying in our own (lack of) power and (in)competence?

Or will we turn to God and move forward in his power and competence?

In a sense, letting go and handing our lives to God

may seem challenging or daunting, maybe even beyond us.

But it's not.

In fact, we might just find it's the most natural thing we'll ever do.

Why?

Because we are God's children, so it makes total sense to give our lives to him.

WHY YOU DO WHAT YOU DO

WHAT YOU DO IS determined by what you think of you.

But that's *not* why you think you do what you do.

You think you weigh pros and cons.

You think you do what makes you happy.

You think you try to do what's right.

No. What you do is determined by what you think of you.

And what you think of you probably isn't true.

No, Timer: You Aren't What You Eat

When I was a kid, in between weekend cartoons, the network would show "Saturday Morning Brain Food" public service announcements featuring "Timer." Timer was an animated character who looked kind of like an ugly lemon come to life with a big pocket watch and a bigger nose. Timer would sing songs like "I Hanker for a Hunk of

Cheese," teaching kids that cheese-and-cracker sandwiches make for a nutritious snack.*

I'm not sure about Timer's grasp of human health.

In another commercial he taught us kids that we are what we eat, singing, "All these motors in your body need a lot of fuel to go on, like carbohydrates, fats and proteins, vitamins, and so on. What's left over forms the building blocks you need, indeed, to grow on." Um, I'm pretty sure the proteins and vitamins and such *are* the building blocks we need. What's "left over" is *not* building blocks. What's left over is, well, you know, poop.

But what I really take issue with is Timer's assertion that you are what you eat. I realize that what we put into our bodies is important, but what we are is what we believe in our minds—specifically what we believe about ourselves.

Well, that may not be exactly what we are. But what we believe about ourselves, our self-identity, *does* dominate how we act and relate to other people and do our jobs and, well, basically everything.

Here's a way the Bible says it: "As he thinks within himself, so he is."[1]

Or: what you do is determined by what you think of you.

You don't have to believe the Bible to believe that. Check this: social scientists study why people make the decisions they do.

- Why do you spend extra to get a better brand of hot dogs but buy the cheapest gas?
- Why do you feel like you have to dress a little nicer than everyone else at social functions?
- Why do you vote Republican or Democrat?

Though some decision making is based on analyzing costs and benefits, it turns out that more often we make choices based on what

---

* Duh. Of course a chunk of saturated fat sitting on a little edible plate of carbohydrates is good for you. We didn't need Timer to figure that out.

James March describes as the identity model.[2] March, a professor at Stanford University, says that when making a decision, we essentially (and subconsciously) ask ourselves three questions:

- Who am I?
- What kind of situation is this?
- What would someone like me do in this situation?

Or, in other words, what you do is determined by what you think of you.

This helps explain why a self-employed shrimper in Alabama would vote *against* a Democrat who would give him health insurance and why a Hollywood millionaire would vote *against* a Republican who would cut her taxes. Neither choice makes sense if we make decisions based on self-interest. But if what we do is based on our self-perceived identity, each choice makes all the sense in the world.

What you do is determined by what you think of you.

Research demonstrates the enormous power of identity in decision making.

For instance, two Stanford University psychologists in the 1960s performed a study where they went door-to-door asking people for permission to put a "Drive Carefully" billboard in their front yards.[3] A picture was shown to the residents. The billboard was poorly constructed and so large it would pretty much take up the entire front yard, blocking the front of their house. Eighty-three percent of the homeowners said no.[†]

Let me interrupt the story with a quick question: Why do you think they said no?

You think it was because of self-interest. They quickly weighed the pros and cons and came to the obvious decision that there was not enough benefit to outweigh the costs. Why do you think that?

[†] What I want to know is: Who are the 17 percent who said yes? For real?!

Because you believe decisions are made by assessing pros and cons. As we'll see, believing that is part of our problem.

Back to the story . . .

In a nearby neighborhood, two weeks prior, the researchers had people go door-to-door claiming to represent an organization dedicated to driver safety. They asked residents to put a small "Be a Safe Driver" sign in the windows of their cars or homes. Almost all agreed. Two weeks later the two Stanford University psychologists showed up and made the same request they had in the other neighborhood: Would the homeowner be willing to put a huge, crudely made "Drive Carefully" billboard in their front yard? *Seventy-six percent* of the people in this second neighborhood said yes!

Why? The researchers concluded that agreeing to put the small card in their windows shifted the homeowners' sense of identity. That one act led them to become, in their own eyes, the kind of people who do that kind of thing. They were concerned citizens who were committed to preventing others from encountering or creating dangerous situations. That newly formed identity led them to a different answer to the request of having an obnoxious billboard put in their front yard. When asked, they subconsciously went through the same series of questions we all do when faced with a decision: Who am I? What kind of situation is this? What would someone like me do in this situation?

How Do We Change What We Do?

This is critical for us to grasp if we're ever going to change. Our attempts at transformation typically take the form of behavior modification:

- "I'm going to quit smoking on January 1!"
- "That's it. I will never look at porn again!"
- "This year I'm going to eat healthy and exercise every day!"
- "I'm going to stop dating men who are mean to me. In fact, I'm not going to date at all for a while!"

- "I'm going to read the Bible every morning this whole year!"
- "I'm not going to exaggerate or lie or gossip to get attention or feel better about myself. No more!"

The problem is we realize we need to change, based on a cost-benefit analysis of our behavior, so we make the commitment. But our decisions are *not* based on cost-benefit analyses, so we won't *keep* the commitment. Our decisions are based on our perceived identities, and if our identities don't change, we will eventually go back to the same behaviors.

So getting unstuck (finally stopping this or starting that) *won't* happen because we try to change our *behaviors*; it *will* happen when we change our *identities*.

What you do is determined by what you think of you.

And what you think of you probably isn't true.

There's good news: we can change our self-perception. We can change our identity.

*   *   *

If you aren't already part of TheRestoreCommunity.com—what are you waiting for? It's a free place to dive deeper into the things we're talking about. Watch videos, download a free PDF journal, and interact with other people on the same journey as you!

THE TOP TEN TEMPTATIONS
I CAN'T SEEM TO SHAKE

10. Driving around my neighborhood while ringing an ice cream truck bell, then just watching all the disappointed little faces.

9. Binge watching *Gilmore Girls* on Netflix.

8. Binge watching *anything* on Netflix!

7. Throwing tortilla chips at "salsa" dancers.

6. Standing in the cereal aisle and shouting, "I am the secret love child of Captain Crunch!"

5. Stalking my mail carrier, dressed as a German shepherd.

4. Removing the tag from the mattress.

3. Wearing my "Members Only" jacket.

2. Giving children Red Vines and telling them they're Twizzlers.

1. Writing stupid top ten lists.

I KNOW I AM, BUT WHO AM I?

THE EARTHQUAKE REGISTERED 7.9 on the Richter scale. Massive. Almost ninety thousand people died in the Sichuan province in China.

Thirty students were sitting in their second grade classroom when the earthquake hit. The school building collapsed on the students. Some of the second graders died instantly. Most were injured and unconscious. Those who were able climbed out of the rubble and ran from the building.

Except one.

Nine-year-old Lin Hao was the first to get out, but then he did something none of the other escapees did. He went back. He went back into the rubble and pulled one of his unconscious classmates out to safety. Then he went back in and rescued another classmate. Rubble fell on him as he made his dashes back into the school, injuring his arms and head. That didn't stop him. Nothing stopped him. When there was no one left to rescue, Lin Hao encouraged the nine surviving classmates to sing songs to keep their spirits up as they waited for help.

Why did Lin Hao do what he did?

"I was the hall monitor. It was my job to look after my classmates." His behavior was driven by his identity.

What you do is determined by what you think of you.

Mo

I once got a fortune cookie message that said, "When sheep are your only companions, a burning bush will get your attention."

Okay—I lied. I never got that in a fortune cookie. It just seemed like a cool way to introduce Moses' story.*

Moses grew up in Egypt, the adopted son of Pharaoh. Pharaoh was the most powerful man in the world. Moses knew that, by birth, he was a Hebrew. The Hebrews were the people Pharaoh held in slavery. One day Moses saw a Hebrew slave being abused, and he killed the abuser in a fit of rage. Afraid for his life, Moses skipped town. Eventually he got a job tending sheep.

That's when Moses saw the burning bush. As my Chinese restaurant dessert predicted, he went over to check it out. It spoke.[1]

Moses wasn't used to hearing plants speak, so he asked the bush to identify itself. God said that he was God. Moses, who grew up in the Egyptian palace where all kinds of gods were worshiped, asked God to be more specific. God told him he is the one true God. He even let Moses know his name. He said his name is I Am.

God told Moses about his future. It wasn't the kind of vague message you'll find in a fortune cookie.† God told Moses he had heard the cry of the Hebrew people. He was going to set them free. Specifically, he wanted Moses to lead them to freedom.

Moses looked God right in the eye‡ and said *no*.

---

* And I love Chinese food!

† "You are about to receive good news from a friend!" "Your lucky numbers: 7, 17, 4, 9."

‡ Well, to be more precise, I guess he looked God right in the flaming leaf.

Why did Moses say no?

The same reason we do what we do: what he thought of himself.

In fact, Moses says to God, repeatedly, "Who am I?" "Who am I to do this?" "Who am I?"

Moses had gone from thinking he was the prince of Egypt to thinking he was a fugitive murderer turned shepherd.

Does it make any sense for a fugitive murderer shepherd to represent God and make demands of the king? No, it does not. Why did Moses say no? Because what you do is determined by what you think of you.

Why should Moses have immediately said yes?

Because he *wasn't* who he thought he was. Moses *had* murdered someone. He *had* run away. He *was* living as a fugitive. His job *was* herding sheep. But that's *not* who Moses was.

Moses' problem was an identity crisis.

He had just met God. He was now on a *first-name basis* with God. He knew God but didn't really know himself.

If you had asked Moses, I think he would have told you . . .

"I know I Am, but who am I?"

You

Why do you do what you do? Why do you . . .

- spend too much time at work and not enough time with your family?
- only feel good about yourself if a guy is paying attention to you?
- have angry outbursts that are disproportionate to the situation?
- spend all your time on social media, ignoring real people who need your attention?
- eat a half gallon of ice cream when you're depressed?
- look at porn even though you swore you never would again?

- feel like you're important only if others view you as successful?
- not feel successful even if everyone else views you that way?
- sabotage every romantic relationship you have?

Because what you do is determined by what you think of you.

Why *shouldn't* you be doing what you're doing? (Or why should you be doing what you're not doing?)

Because you're not who you think you are.

You may have done all of those things, but that's *not* who you are.

You may know God, but my guess is you don't know yourself.

Your problem is an identity crisis. You have a false ID.

False ID

We like to think we're self-made, that we've set our own course, but the truth is we are amalgamations of the messages we've received. What we believe about ourselves is largely based on what we've been told about ourselves. Humans are like sponges, soaking in those messages. Those messages form our identity, our sense of who we are.

We don't necessarily take in every message. We tend to receive messages from sources we view as credible: parents, teachers, and friends, or maybe the bully at school, grandparents, or a coach.

A pioneer in sociology named Charles Cooley coined the phrase "looking-glass self." "Looking glass" is an old-timey name for mirrors. Cooley said what you believe others think of you is like the mirror you look in and will become how you see yourself.

Those messages from others especially impact you if you receive them early in life or often in life. If you receive them early *and* often, those messages can tattoo you psychologically with indelible ink.

I received the message early and often from my father: "You're not good enough." "You can't figure things out." "You mess everything up." "You are really, really stupid."

Those messages defined what I thought of me.

I've spent my life trying to prove I'm intelligent, and I'm afraid people will realize I'm not as smart as they think I am.

I worked my butt off in college to get straight As but hoped people wouldn't realize I had to work hard. I got a full-ride academic scholarship to law school but still didn't feel smart. Ever since, I've noticed that I'll find ways to nonchalantly mention I went to law school. Why? I'm trying to prove I'm not stupid. But, honestly, I'm sure I am.

It's not just that I feel stupid. I feel unlovable, unworthy of being loved. Of course I do. My father was obligated to love me, and he couldn't do it. Why would someone else *choose* to love me? In fact, when my wife says, "I love you," it makes me uncomfortable. Something inside me flinches.

So, who tattooed you?

What message did you receive?

- "You're only important if you're in the spotlight."
- "You'll never amount to much."
- "You're not pretty enough because you're not thin. You need to watch your weight."
- "Men will always hurt you."
- "You're impossible."

Your problem is an identity crisis. You have a false ID. What you believe about yourself is largely based on what you've been told about yourself.

There may be other identity-forming factors. Sometimes we try to form false identities to prove other false identity messages wrong.

You might define yourself by your performance. You introduce yourself by your job title. That's no mistake. In your mind, you are what you do. Who are you? Read your résumé.

Or you might define yourself by your sin. You screwed up, had a blowout. Maybe it was bad. It was big. Or maybe it's been repeated—a lot. You can't get past it. In fact, your sin has become the mirror you see yourself in.

Your problem? You aren't who you think you are.

Symptoms

Your problem is that you aren't who you think you are. The trouble is, that's not what you think your problem is.

You think it's gossiping. Or being obsessively controlling. Or always ending up with guys who are mean to you. Or spending money you can't afford to spend. Or lusting. Or needing two glasses of wine every night to calm your nerves. Or being overbearing with your kids.

You've probably tried to solve that problem. But the reason you can't solve that problem is because that problem *isn't* your problem. It's a *symptom* of your problem.

Your problem is that what you do is determined by what you think of you, and you're not who you think you are.

So the way to solve your problem is for you to get a new identity.

You need to get your *true* identity.

DAY 13

TRUTH FROM THE ATTIC

My MOTHER SAT DOWN AT the kitchen table holding something that would change my life forever. I was fifteen and about to discover I wasn't who I thought I was.

Growing up, I had a vague sense that something was not right about my name. I was never sure why I felt that way.

Finally, the answer came out. Actually, the answer came *down* from my mother's attic. She was holding a document. Before showing it to me, she shared the circumstances of my birth.

When I was born, my father thought the FBI was after him. Believing he couldn't register at the hospital under his real name (Vincent Antonucci), he registered under and then gave me the name Vincent Shuffle.* Later he had a fake birth certificate made for me with the name Vincent Antonucci. I was always told my name was

---

* As a "professional" poker player, he must have thought "Shuffle" was funny.

Vincent Antonucci, and my parents had used my fake birth certificate my whole life.

At the kitchen table, my mother showed me my actual birth certificate and suggested that I file for a name change and make my legal name Vincent Antonucci. It was the only name I had ever known. We did the paperwork and went to see a judge, and suddenly I had a new, but old, name. In a sense it was a new identity, but all along it had really been my true identity.

The Problem behind the Problems

When my wife and I showed up at the hospital for the birth of our first child, unlike my parents, I did not believe I was wanted by the FBI. We registered under our actual names, and a few hours later our son was born. No aliases necessary. We named him Dawson.

The next day, Dawson had a high temperature. He was dehydrated. The doctors were confused, fearing meningitis and later a heart complication. For seven days we remained in the hospital as they watched him closely and ran a battery of tests.

Finally, on a Tuesday, they gave him a clean bill of health and sent us home. Wednesday afternoon my wife was shaking uncontrollably on our couch with a high temperature. Thursday morning she was admitted back into the hospital with a mysterious uterine infection and a 104.7 temperature. She and Dawson spent the next five days back in the hospital together. Jen kept getting worse.

Finally they figured out what was wrong. The doctor came in and explained that after the baby was delivered, a tiny speck of the placenta had been left in Jen. Her body detected this "foreign body" and was attacking it. All the problems we had seen were actually just symptoms.

Who Are You?

You may not have a false name, but you *do* have a false identity.

Your false identity leads to your other problems.

Your other problems are really just symptoms of your true problem. What will fix your problem is a new identity.

What you need is your *true* identity.

So who are you? Not who you think you are. Not who your parents said you are. Not what the kids at school make you feel like you are. No—who are you? Really?

You are a child of God. Don't read that in a cute-needlepoint-on-a-wall, what-old-ladies-at-church-might-say, what-you-heard-in-a-cheesy-Christian-song kind of way. Read it like it's the truest thing you've ever read, because it is. Read it like it's the most important, liberating, transforming truth you've ever read, because it is. All you have to do is say yes to God's offer to adopt you, through your putting your faith in Jesus, and . . . you are a child of God.*

There is a God, who is the reason behind it all—the beginning and end of why everything exists, who is bigger and better than anything else, who is all powerful and all loving, and *you are God's child.*

What does that mean?

It means you are valuable and lovable.

My birth certificate wasn't the only life-changing thing that came down from my mom's attic. Years later I was visiting, and my mother announced it was time for me to take my childhood things she had been saving for me. She brought down a box from the attic—LEGOs, Matchbox cars, books, and . . . a teddy bear.

It was *my* teddy bear from when I was little. It was a mess. My mother had sewn an ear back on. She had done reconstructive surgery on its neck and back. It was missing fur around its eyes, on both feet, and on its back by the little music handle. There was a big scar across its head. The cutest thing was the four little pieces of fur missing from where my four fingers used to hold it constantly. My finger marks had become permanently embedded in my bear.

---

* See, for instance, John 1:12-13, NIV: "Yet to all who did receive him, to those who believed in his name, he gave the right to become children of God—children born not of natural descent, nor of human decision or a husband's will, but born of God."

When I was little, I *loved* this bear, but there was nothing lovable, nothing valuable about the bear in itself. Even when it was new, it was obviously not an expensive stuffed animal. It probably cost a few dollars at the time. If you tried to sell it at a garage sale today, you might ask for a dime. It's just not valuable—except that it is to *me*, and it especially was when I was a kid.

I loved this bear. But I didn't love it because it was valuable. I loved it because . . . I loved it. I loved it because it was *my* bear. My love was not based on its value; rather my love *made* this bear valuable. My love gave this bear significance. When I was a kid, I wouldn't have let my parents sell it at a garage sale for a million dollars.

As an adult, I held that bear and understood how God could love me when I wasn't worth loving. I realized the love I had for my bear is the same kind of love God has for me. It's not a love that loves *because* the object of the love is valuable; it's a love that *gives* value.

God knows me. He knows what I was worth in the beginning. He knows the damage that has been done to me over the years. He knows my current condition. But the most significant thing God knows about me is that I am *his*. I may have been beat up, pulled out of shape, ripped, and left with stuffing hanging out, but I am his. I may not look like much to anyone else, but I am his. So he loves me, and his love gives me value. It makes me lovable.

The same is true for you. Your true identity is that you are a child of God, and that means you are valuable and lovable.

It means you don't have to be perfect.

I have two kids, and I love them. I loved them the moment they were born. They hadn't done anything to prove their value or make themselves lovable, but I loved them. I'm going to be honest: I don't love anyone else's kids. I just love mine. I love them *because* they're mine.

There's nothing they can do to lose that. When they were born, I didn't take them in my arms, gaze into their little cute baby eyes, and say, "Don't blow this. I'm serious! If you screw this up, if you disobey me, if you cause problems, it's over!" No, I love those kids uncondi-tionally. They don't have to be perfect to keep my love. In fact, I don't expect them to be perfect.

Like, I don't want to make them look bad, but when they first started walking, they were terrible at it. I'm serious. They'd pull their little, pudgy twelve-month-old bodies up into a standing position, start wobbling, take a step, and then crash to the ground. I never yelled, "What's wrong with you? Do you see me falling? No, you don't! Since I can walk, and you're my kid, you should be able to do this too. Actually, that's it. I don't need this frustration anymore!" No, they were kids, and I expected them to fall down. Because they were *my* kids, I loved them even when they fell down. I picked them up, put them back on their feet, and smiled as they tried again.

You are God's child. That means you don't have to be perfect. God loves you unconditionally. He expects you to fall down, loves you anyway, and will help you get back up and take your next step. You live in God's grace.

It means you can change.

What you do is determined by what you think of you.

When you realize you are God's child, it will change what you do.

When you put your faith in Jesus, the Bible says you are now "in Christ." It also says, "If anyone is in Christ, he is a new creation. The old has passed away; behold, the new has come."[1]

Imagine a caterpillar crawling around in the mud. Why does a cat-erpillar crawl around in the mud? Because it's a caterpillar. It doesn't have much of a choice; that's its nature.

Now picture that caterpillar going through a metamorphosis and becoming a butterfly. It is now a new creation: the old has gone, the new is here. What will the butterfly do? It will fly. Why does a but-terfly fly? Because it's a butterfly. Flying is part of its nature.

But what if you saw a butterfly crawling around in the mud? What would you assume about that butterfly? Somehow it still thinks it's a caterpillar! Something didn't click to register the new, true identity. A butterfly who knows it's a butterfly wouldn't choose life in the mud now that it can rise above it.

Imagine *you*. Imagine there's some sense in which you've been crawling around in the mud. It may not be hard to imagine:

- Hunting and pecking around the Internet for hours, knowing it will take you places you shouldn't go
- Jealousy of your friends, whom you bad-mouth behind their backs
- A fantasy life where you're married to someone who isn't your actual spouse
- Feeling lonely so you order a pizza and then eat the whole thing by yourself

Why do you do what you do? Because of what you think of you. In your mind, what you're doing is natural, normal. It's who you've always been.

There's a problem. That's *not* who you are. You are a new creation. You are loved and valuable and beautiful and honorable. I know that about you because you are a child of God. When *you* know that about you, what you've been doing won't feel natural or normal. As you focus on your new, true identity, you'll stop choosing to crawl around in the mud. Instead, you'll rise above it.

You are God's child. Accept it. Perhaps you've never known that or have never lived that way. Fine. Then starting today, claim it as your new identity. But it's always been your true identity. You've never done anything to screw that up or lose that. God created you in his image; he created you as his child, and no matter what you've done, it has always been true. God's finger marks are permanently embedded in you.

You are God's child. That is your new, true identity.

There are some other things that are also true of you if you are in Christ:

- *You are a friend of Jesus.*[2] God doesn't just love you; he likes you. He calls you his friend.
- *You are forgiven of all your sins.*[3] If you've said yes to God's offer of forgiveness through Jesus, your sins were wiped away and no longer count against you.
- *You are more than a conqueror.*[4] You are not a victim. You are not helpless. You are not hopeless. Because of Jesus you can conquer anything—and then some.
- *You are God's workmanship.*[5] The word translated "workmanship" in Ephesians is the same word used for poetry. What is poetry? Poetry is when you take a bunch of words, then you get rid of the wrong words, and you put the right words together in the right way, and you make something beautiful. That's what God wants to do in your life! He wants to take all of it, then help you get rid of the wrong things and start putting everything back together in just the right way and make your life something beautiful.

There are a lot of things that have been true of your identity, but maybe you haven't been living in them.

What you do is determined by what you think of you, and you're not who you think you are.

It's time to embrace your true identity.

You are a child of God.

And that means everything.

Shaking like a Leaf

Knowing who you are—that you are a child of God—means everything.

That's why, as a parent, my number-one priority is to help my kids establish their true identities as God's children. I decided to steal a line from the apostle John, who wrote the book of John in the Bible. There's this odd thing John does. Jesus had twelve core disciples.

John repeatedly calls one of them "the disciple Jesus loved" or sometimes "the one Jesus loved." John was referring to himself. It's kind of odd but very cool. I don't think John was insinuating that Jesus loved him more. I think John was so amazed by the fact that Jesus loved him at all that it overwhelmed him. He had trouble thinking of himself as John anymore, or as a fisherman, or as a guy with a hot temper. No, John now knew who he was. His new, true identity was the one Jesus loved.

I decided to try to make that my kids' self-identities. The first thing I would say to them, when the doctor handed them to me, would be, "Do you know who you are? You are the one Jesus loves." The thing I would say to them the most throughout their lives: "You are the one Jesus loves."

If they always identify themselves as "the one Jesus loves," it will change everything for them. Because what you do is determined by what you think of you.

What I've realized is that despite having occasional epiphany moments when I realize I'm a child of God, it's a challenge for me to really think of myself that way.

Remember how my wife and newborn son had to go back to the hospital because my wife had a crazy high fever and was losing control of her body? Eventually the doctors figured out what was wrong, but one night before that, Jen's temperature spiked back up over 104 degrees. She was shaking so bad, it was like she was vibrating. A nurse ran in and tried to get her temperature down. She called for help, and suddenly there were several nurses all working feverishly to get her fever down. I stood against the wall, watching the scene in front of me, freaking out inside. I felt out of control and desperately alone.

Finally, Jen's temperature came down a little, and the nurses left. I was about to start yelling things like "Why is this happening? This is crazy! What if they can't figure out what's wrong?" when Jen said, "I know I'm going to be okay."

"What?" I asked her. "Why? How can you know that?"

"Because," she answered, "while all that was happening, I was singing a song to God, and he just kind of let me know he's here and that he loves us."

Trying to keep my eye roll to a minimum, I asked what she was singing. She sang it. Still shaking, she sang a song by a guy named Rich Mullins: "Hold me Jesus, 'cause I'm shaking like a leaf. You have been King of my glory; won't you be my Prince of peace?"

I looked at her and realized, *That's what it looks like to know you're God's child.*

I looked at myself and realized, *This is* not *what it looks like to know you're God's child.*

So, if I knew I was a child of God, why wasn't I living it?

THE TOP TEN SIGNS YOU SHOULD BE READING A DIFFERENT BOOK

10. You're still wondering where the recipes are.

9. You thought it was a Bible study on Rahab.

8. There aren't enough things to color.

7. You don't speak English.

6. You're allergic to authors whose names rhyme with "Wince Smantonucci."

5. When you think of something to get a fire going, you think of this book.

4. You keep thinking you should just wait and see the movie.

3. You're disappointed by the lack of pictures.

2. You've fallen asleep three times just while trying to get through this top ten list.

1. You've spent the last three hours trying to find Waldo.

CLOTHES OFF. CLOTHES ON.

How many times in a row can you wear the same shirt on a weekly date with your wife before she notices? I still don't know, because after nine times, I finally told her.

Why would I wear the same shirt on a weekly date with my wife? Because she hates the shirt, of course.

It all started one day when I wore the shirt and she said, "I really don't like that shirt. You should throw it out."

We have a date every Friday, when we do romantic things like go to museums and restaurants and Walmart. The Friday after her shirt comment I wore the shirt. I thought she'd find it hysterical, or annoying, which *I* would have found hysterical. She didn't notice. So I wore the shirt the following Friday, and the next, and the Friday after that. One time she said, "Oh, I really hate that shirt." But she didn't acknowledge that I was wearing it on our date or that I had worn it on the previous four dates, so I kept putting it on every Friday. The ninth time in a row she said, "You still haven't thrown out that shirt?"

I couldn't contain myself anymore. "I've worn this shirt nine dates in a row. It's been over two months since we've had a date when I didn't wear this shirt you hate."

She thought it was hysterical.

Then she threw out the shirt.

Ready for the real comedy? *She's* the one who bought me that shirt. It was a present from her.

That was about two years ago. About two months ago we were walking through a department store in a mall and saw a huge sale: 40 percent off men's shirts' sale prices, which were already marked down 50 percent! I'm no Stephen Hawking, but it seemed like a lot of percents. I grabbed about seven shirts, and Jen followed me to the fitting room.

I put one on and came out of the dressing room. Jen looked at me and said, "No."

I put on the second. Jen checked me out and said, "Yes!"

The third got a no.

Finally, I was done trying on the shirts, put the shirt I had been wearing back on, and walked out of the fitting room. Jen looked me over and said, "No!"

"This is my shirt," I protested, "the one I've been wearing all day."

"Oh," Jen laughed. "Sorry, I don't like it."

Ready for more comedy? She bought me *that* shirt too! It was another present she gave me.

I guess the lesson is that my wife really doesn't like her taste in clothing.

Muscle Memory

So why did I know I was God's child but have trouble remembering it and living like it?

I think the answer has to do with clothes (which I'll get back to in a minute), and also with chickens.

I must admit that I'm no expert on chickens, except for eating them.* I have not spent a lot of time with chickens except when they're on my plate. But there is something I know about chickens. If you cut a chicken's head off, it will run around like . . . a chicken with its head cut off.

Why does a chicken, without a brain to send signals to its body, continue to run around? Muscle memory.† The brain has been sending messages to the chicken's body for so long, the body can continue to function for a while without new input, based on the old messages.

So why did I know I was God's child but continue to run around like I was unlovable and had to prove myself to the world? Let's call it muscle memory. Those messages had been playing in my head for so long, they were continuing to send the same signals.

But He Ain't Yoda

A few years ago my church management team told me Jen and I should go see Obi-Wan Kenobi. Well, not *actually* Obi-Wan Kenobi, but they made him sound like it. In fact, everyone did. He was a counselor to pastors with struggling marriages who could say some magic Jedi words and the couple would start making out like newlyweds.

I told my management team my marriage wasn't struggling. They said it would still be a smart preventative measure. I agreed—*begrudgingly*. First, I went to sex addiction rehab without having a sex addiction (I still need to tell you what happened with that), and now I was going to struggling marriage rehab without having a struggling marriage.

We flew to Colorado for our week of marriage therapy. On the first day, Obi-Wan (who turned out to have a PhD but no lightsaber)

---

* There's not a lot you can say that about without getting weird looks. Try it. Like, "I'm not an expert on horses, except for eating them." "I'm not an expert on toilet plungers, except for eating them." "I'm not an expert on Donald Trump, except for eating him."

† But please remember I'm no expert on chickens, so don't quote me on that.

said our marriage was great, and I was the one with issues, not Jen. I told Dr. Kenobi that Jen didn't like her own taste in clothing. He acted like that was irrelevant and gave her the rest of the week off.

Over the next four days we talked about my issue. My issue was my identity. I still thought of myself as unlovable. The voice that dominated my thoughts about myself was my earthly father's, not my heavenly Father's. I told Dr. Kenobi it didn't make sense, because I'd had the epiphany. I knew I am the one Jesus loves. I had a scraggly teddy bear to prove it.

He explained this wasn't a one-time epiphany kind of deal. It was a war. My father had so repeatedly tattooed me with the stupid, unlovable identity, and I had thought of myself that way for so long, that those thoughts wouldn't just go away on their own. I would have to fight against them. We looked at a passage in the Bible:

For though we live in the world, we do not wage war as the world does. The weapons we fight with are not the weapons of the world. On the contrary, they have divine power to demolish strongholds. We demolish arguments and every pretension that sets itself up against the knowledge of God, and we take captive every thought to make it obedient to Christ.[1]

I learned that in ancient times every city had a stronghold. A stronghold was a fortress built on top of the highest point in the city. It was basically impenetrable. It was used to protect leaders if the city was attacked.

Dr. Kenobi told me we have mental strongholds, fortresses we've built that we've made impenetrable to God. They're our high places, in that we've elevated them to a higher position than God. We think we've created them for our protection, but the truth is that these strongholds become prisons. We think they help us have control, but they actually control us.

Strongholds are ways of thinking that run counter to God's truth, and we need to take those thoughts captive and make them obedient to Christ. We need to battle to let the truth of God overwhelm the lies we believe.

The lie I believed was that I'm unlovable because I'm no good.

The truth is that I am loved because I'm God's child.

Just like someone with a drug addiction doesn't have an epiphany that drugs are bad and is never tempted by drugs again, my epiphany that I am the one Jesus loves wasn't enough. I would be tempted every day to go back to my old identity. I would have to demolish that pretension, that lie.

Obi-Wan showed me another passage in the Bible he thought would help. It is about taking off and putting on clothes.* It starts,

Since, then, you have been raised with Christ, set your hearts on things above, where Christ is, seated at the right hand of God. Set your minds on things above, not on earthly things. For you died, and your life is now hidden with Christ in God.[2]

My Jedi Master told me the idea was that I died (spiritually) and started a new life with God. I died to my old identity. My *new* identity is now with Jesus.

He pointed out the instruction to "set your hearts" and "set your minds." Those were things *I* had to do.

In the next few verses is another command: "Put to death, therefore, whatever belongs to your earthly nature." Then a reminder: "You used to walk in these ways, in the life you once lived."[3]

The passage then gets into the clothes part: "You have taken off your old self with its practices and have put on the new self, which is being renewed in knowledge in the image of its Creator."[4]

The idea, according to Dr. Kenobi, is that our original identity is

---

* Which made me kind of mad. He said my wife's issue with my shirts was irrelevant, but now he's bringing up clothes?!

that we are loved children of God, and that our true identity has been restored. Now we have to start living it. We need to "take off," to *stop* doing, the kinds of things that were part of our old identity. Then we need to "put on," to *start* doing, the kinds of things that are part of our new identity:

> Therefore, as God's chosen people, holy and dearly loved, clothe yourselves with compassion, kindness, humility, gentleness and patience. Bear with each other and forgive one another if any of you has a grievance against someone. Forgive as the Lord forgave you. And over all these virtues put on love, which binds them all together in perfect unity.[5]

Just like every day I take off and put on clothes, I have to make the choice every day to take off my old identity and put on my new, true identity.

Then Obi-Wan gave me an assignment to do that night before coming back in the morning. I was excited to work on my Jedi mind-trick skills, but that wasn't the assignment. My homework was to write a letter about me, to me, from God. I had heard lies about me for so long that I needed to hear the truth about me.

"It would be pretty weird," I told him, "to write to me, about me, from God."

"Don't worry about weird," he said. "Just do it." He didn't wave his hand in front of my face, and I wasn't convinced.

"How do I know what God would say about me?"

He was starting to look a little annoyed. "You know. You know what the Bible says."

"Well, fine"—I wasn't going down without a fight—"but my letter will just be me stringing Bible verses together."

He said that was fine. (I think at this point he was just trying to get rid of me.)

I left, and I wrote the letter.

The next day he had me read it out loud in front of him. (Awkward!) He said it was great and that I should read it every morning. It was part of demolishing the stronghold, of taking off my old identity and putting on the new.

I later read a book on addictive thinking called *Addictive Thinking*.* The author wrote that addictive thinking is always irrational thinking. Addicts are irrational, at least in the area of their addiction. Therefore, they will not come to the truth on their own. The source of rational thinking must come from outside the addict.[6]

I realized Dr. Kenobi was right. I could never convince myself I was living with the wrong identity. There were too many years of irrational, addictive thinking. To put on my new, true identity, I needed an outside source. So I kept reading my letter from God,† and it definitely started helping.

But it didn't fully do the trick. Strongholds are hard to destroy.

That's when Dr. Kenobi came to my town.

More Outside Sources

I received an e-mail that Obi-Wan would be in Las Vegas and could see me if I had some time.

I had some time.

We met, and I told him reading the letter was definitely helping, but I was still struggling a little to take off my old identity. We talked and came up with an idea.

To get more outside input, I would ask some close friends to write me a short letter. I believed the lie that I am unlovable, so I would ask them to tell me why I *am* lovable. I knew the answer was that I'm God's child, but was there anything else good about me?

It turns out asking friends to write a letter to me about me was just as awkward as writing a letter to me about me from God. But I

---

* No points for a clever title.
† Well, at least all the Bible verses in it are from God. If you'd like to see my letter, I've put it in the back of this book (page 271).

did it anyway. I asked some friends, and they wrote me letters about me. Reading them was transformational.

Now, in ways I couldn't before, I can tell you some good things about me. That might not sound exciting, but a few years ago if you had asked me to tell you everything good about me, I would have said, "Um, well, I'm kind of funny. And I can get my money's worth at an all-you-can-eat buffet," and that would have been it. I would have been serious.

Ask me now.

I'm the one Jesus loves.

Because I'm God's Child . . .

There's a path out of our problem. The second step of that path is this: *Because I'm God's child, I give my life to his will.*

If we're going to get past our past and become healthy and whole, we have to do that.

But to do that, you have to really think of yourself as God's child. Because what you do is determined by what you think of you. If you've been tattooed with a different identity, you can get to a place where you think of yourself as God's child. It won't happen by an epiphany. It will be the battle of your life. But it's a battle you can win when, with God's help, you start taking every thought captive, taking off the old and putting on the new.

When you do, your life will change.

Changing my identity changed my life.

But to change my life, *my* identity wasn't the only one I had to change.

I had to change what I thought of someone else, too.

GOD ISN'T WHO YOU THINK HE IS

SHE CAME BOUNCING UP right when our church service ended.

"Hey! Hi! My name's Sandy," she said very quickly, "but not for long it isn't. I'm changing it! It's been a bad year for Sandys—Hurricane Sandy, Sandy Hook Elementary."

I tried to respond, but no chance.

"So, hey!" Sandy cut me off, "I just wanted to thank you for keeping it positive."

I started to ask what she meant but didn't need to.

"I went to church a few times growing up," Sandy speed-talked, "and I've gone a couple times as an adult, and I hate it. Hate it! You always feel like you're being judged. People look down on you. It's all negative. It's all about their rules. 'Don't do this. Don't do that.' They tell me I have to dress appropriately. I've always hated church, but I've always wanted to know Jesus. So when I heard about this church, I decided I would check it out one time, and it was great! Thanks for keeping it positive. I'll be back next week!"

As I got to know Sandy over the next few weeks, I learned that the way she had been treated in church bled over into the way she thought about God. She assumed he was always judging and looking down on her, that he was always negative.

The Most Important Thing about You

So I thought he invented root beer—sue me.

It turns out A. W. Tozer wasn't Mr. A&W himself; he was a theologian who probably knew nothing about root beer but had some good things to say about God. Here's one of them: "What comes into our minds when we think about God is the most important thing about us."[1]

He's right.

He's right, among other reasons, because we need to hand our lives over to God. That's the second step in our path to healing and freedom and wholeness: *Because I'm God's child, I give my life to his will.*

We need to give our lives to God because that's what we were made for. And we need to because that's the only way life will work. And we need to because that's the only way we'll get better.

We need to.

But will we?

It depends. It depends partly on what you think of you and a lot on what you think of God.

God Is . . . Perfect and Powerful

How can we really know what God is like? It would seem that, at best, we could form misty notions and best guesses. I mean, God is way different from us and far removed from us. He's up there, and we're down here.

That's part of the reason God sent Jesus. Jesus came and hung out where we live. Jesus is God, living in our human skin, in our neighborhood. Jesus is an exact representation of God.[2] When you look at Jesus, you see God. And getting an accurate picture of God is the most important thing about us. So we need to take a good look at Jesus.

What do we learn about God from Jesus?

We learn that God is perfect and powerful. We see that in Jesus.

Jesus was perfect. He never sinned. If you want to know someone's sin, there are two people you should ask. You ask that person's enemies, and you ask that person's closest friends. Right? Because enemies are always looking for flaws, and best friends are around enough to see that person at his or her worst. What's interesting is that Jesus' enemies couldn't find anything to accuse him of,[3] and his best friends adamantly proclaimed he was sinless.[4]

Jesus was also powerful. He had power over nature,[5] power in his teaching,[6] power to transform the lives of the people he met.[7]

Jesus was perfect and powerful, and that means *God* is perfect and powerful. I am thankful for that. I could never put my trust in God otherwise. A god who wasn't perfect or wasn't powerful might let me down, might disappoint me. The only kind of god I could give my life to is one who is perfect and powerful. And God is that.

But perfect and powerful isn't enough. I need more. And God is more.

God Is . . . Compassionate and Merciful

What do we learn about God from Jesus?

We learn that God is perfect and powerful. You might expect that. But the surprise bombshell is that God is also compassionate and merciful. We also see that in Jesus.

We see God's compassion and mercy in how Jesus dealt with people.

How do you think God responds to sinners? I'm talking hardcore, committed, caught-in-the-act, unrepentant sinners. Turns out he responds with compassion and mercy. We see that in Jesus.[8]

How do you think God responds to betrayers? I'm talking people who betray God and God's people, who raise money to fund an army that is marching from town to town massacring people who remain faithful to God. Turns out he responds with compassion and mercy. We see that in Jesus.[9]

How do you think God responds to people who live horrible lives, do all kinds of wrong, and then at the last minute make a deathbed confession? Turns out he responds with compassion and mercy. We see that in Jesus.[10]

We also see God's compassion and mercy in what Jesus went through.

God came to earth and lived as a human. If *you* were God and lived as a human, what human life would you choose for yourself? Me, I'd be born in a palace. I'd grow up as royalty, vacation in Hawaii, drive a Lamborghini, and eat only at Brazilian steak houses. Oh, and I'd definitely be born in the age of indoor plumbing.

When God came to earth, what life did he choose?

He was conceived out of wedlock to a teenage mother. Raised in a very religious culture, in a very small town, he would have been known as "that bastard boy."

Growing up, not only was he probably looked down on and ridiculed, it seems he also experienced the death of his earthly father.

Jesus lived in poverty.*

Jesus went out alone into the wilderness, where Satan tempted him repeatedly, attacking Jesus in his most vulnerable places.[11]

Jesus had a close friend who died. As he grieved the loss, family members of the deceased blamed Jesus for the death. He was accused of something that wasn't his fault.[12]

Jesus had what seems to have been a pretty dysfunctional family. Like there's the time, after he had announced that he's the Messiah, when his mother and brothers showed up and told everyone Jesus had lost his mind.[13]

We see Jesus praying with crying and tears.[14] He wrestled with feelings that nearly tore him to pieces. In fact, he had feelings of wanting to die.[15]

Jesus had friends betray and desert him.[16]

Even worse, he felt betrayed and deserted by God.[17]

---

* Toilet paper hadn't even been invented yet.

Remember, all of that is the life God *chose* for himself. Why? Because he is compassionate and merciful. Because God wanted to go through everything we go through. Because he wanted to understand not just the facts of our weaknesses and struggles but also the feelings of our weaknesses and struggles.

That's really important. It's vital because when we think about our temptations and problems, we can view God as the enemy who is responsible for all of it. But what we don't consider is that Jesus went through all the same trials we do. That's why he's described in the Bible as "a man of sorrows and acquainted with grief."[18] Everything we go through, he's gone through. Everything we feel, he's felt.

And That Means . . .

Maybe you've pictured God as distant and unknowable or as demanding and unappeasable.

But that picture isn't right. Because of Jesus, we know that God is so much better than we could have ever imagined or even hoped.

He is perfect and powerful. Thank God for that.

He is also compassionate and merciful.

He loves you and wants to transform your life, and he chose to do it through his own suffering.[19]

He chose to become like us in every way, to go through what we go through, so he could understand our struggles, sympathize with our feelings, and respond with a mercy only possible from someone who's been there and done that.[20]

That means we can "come boldly to the throne of our gracious God. There we will receive his mercy, and we will find grace to help us when we need it most."[21]

It means you can trust him, completely.

It means you can give your life to his will.

We need to know that, and we need to *do* that, because this step is the critical one.

Sandy Strikes Again

Sandy (who I later discovered was a Britney Spears impersonator who sang and danced provocatively in a casino on the Strip) kept coming back to our church, week after week. She didn't change her name and didn't miss a service.

Then there was one I kind of wished she had missed.

The message was on having purity in your marriage. I spent half the sermon talking to our single people. I explained that they could have purity in their marriages *later* by having purity before marriage *now*. So, I taught them not to sleep with anyone until marriage.

I noticed Sandy sitting in the second row. I thought, *She is never coming back after hearing me tell her she can't have sex until she's married. She's gonna say we're another one of those negative churches. I wonder if she's the type to just storm out or if she's the type to come up and let me have it,* then *storm out.*

After the service Sandy immediately walked toward me. I thought, *She's the type to let me have it and then storm out.*

I started to greet her, but nope, no chance.

"Vince," she said immediately. She paused. "I'm getting baptized!"

"Huh?" was all I could get out before she continued.

"Yes! Since coming here my life has completely changed. If I explained it to you, I would start crying." She started crying. "The way I think about *everything* has changed. The way I think about God, myself, life. So I am giving my life to God, and I am getting baptized!"

Sandy got baptized and soon began to change everything about her life—without anyone telling her to. She broke up with her boyfriend. She quit her job.

Later, someone asked how it all happened. She said, "I heard Vince say, 'God has so much love for you.' And I just remember thinking, *I never knew that.* And I felt it for the first time, and it just opened up a whole new life for me."

God has a whole new life for you, too.

You can start living it when, because you're his child, you give your life to his will.

JUMP!

I LOOKED DOWN. Whoa. It was farther than I thought. Way farther. This, I decided, was a bad idea.

Do you remember the first time you went up on the high dive at the pool?

You stood forever in a long line of kids. Finally, it was your turn. You cautiously climbed the rest of the ladder without looking down. You started inching onto the diving board, reached the end, looked down, and realized you did *not* want to do this. This was a mistake. What were you thinking? Then you heard something. A kid's voice. It sounded like one of the kids yelled something. There it was again. It was the word *jump*. Then a different voice, same word, "Jump!" Soon, all the kids are chanting, with great impatience and derision, "Jump! Jump! Jump!"

In our journey to freedom, it's time to jump.

A Muddy Masterpiece

I have a friend named John. He's very smart. He's also really good looking. He's written a *New York Times* bestselling book. I'm not saying I want to poke him in the eye with a stick. But, yes, I want to poke him in the eye with a stick.

This friend John is a pastor, and he has a great illustration that has helped me a lot.[1]

Let's say you were up in your attic. The day you moved into the house, you shoved a few boxes up there and haven't seen the attic since. But another day you find yourself in the attic, and you notice something. It's in the corner. It's not yours; you've never seen it. It must have been left by some previous owner. You go over and realize it's an old painting. You take it out of the attic and, upon inspection, recognize this is a masterpiece by a famous artist. There's only one problem: it has mud splotched all over it. You get on the Internet and discover your new possession is worth millions of dollars.

Would you focus on the mud?

No, you wouldn't. You would focus on the masterpiece! You have a painting worth millions, and your goal would be to get rid of the mud so you can reveal the masterpiece. You might think of trying to do it yourself, but you'd realize that if you were to go at it with a sponge, you might ruin the painting. It would quickly occur to you that the process of removing the mud is too complicated for you. You would bring it to a master, who could remove the mud and restore the painting to its original condition.

God made *you* a masterpiece.

You've gotten some mud on you. You know that. Some of it has been thrown on you. Some of it you've caked on yourself. You're messy.

But that doesn't change your value.

It just means the mud needs to be removed to reveal the masterpiece.

You have a God who is perfect. He knows what he is doing.

You have a God who is compassionate. He understands the mud. He's willing to lovingly and patiently work with you to remove the mud and get you back to your true identity.

You can trust him.

The Core

It's time to give your life over to God's will.

It's time to jump.

This, by the way, is the very core of Christianity.

Becoming a Christian is *not* about just believing in God.[2] It's about surrendering your life to God. Belief without true surrender leads to a life of bleh, and worse.[*]

The twelve-step founders wisely made this one of the steps, the third step. But Jesus made this the very first step: "If any of you wants to be my follower, you must give up your own way, take up your cross daily, and follow me."[3]

God isn't looking for you to add him to your life. That will never work.

God is looking for you to surrender your life to him. That's the only way life will ever work.

The core of Christianity, what it means to become a Christian, is to surrender your life to God.

There's a problem, though. Surrender feels like dying. That's probably why Jesus said we have to "take up our cross." The only reason someone took up a cross was to carry it to his or her execution.

Surrendering to God is how we liberate ourselves, but it feels like dying. Think of a heroin addict making the decision to truly give up heroin. It's the only way he'll ever be free, but it will be the most tortured decision he'll ever make. *Your* baseline addiction is to yourself. Remember, you fired God and took control. You now need to fire

---

[*] Richard Rohr writes, "In fact, I would say what makes so much religion so innocuous, ineffective, and even unexciting is that there has seldom been a concrete 'decision to turn our lives over to the care of God.'" Richard Rohr, *Breathing Under Water: Spirituality and the Twelve Steps* (Cincinnati, OH: St. Anthony Messenger Press, 2011), 20.

yourself and give the job back to God. But handing your life to God, giving up your addiction to you, will feel like dying.

It should.

That death, that surrender, is the core of true Christianity.

It's also the core of recovery. People who oversee rehab centers will tell you it's maybe the most critical step in a successful rehab.

You may not be a follower of Jesus, and you may not be interested in "becoming a Christian."

Still, if you want to put your past in your past, if you want freedom today, if you want to be a healthy, whole person tomorrow, you *must* give your life to his will.

Why?

Because you can't, but God can.

And because you are God's child. When you focus on that, you'll realize nothing is more natural, nothing is more *you*, than handing your life to him.

He's Ready and Waiting

It's time to jump.

As a kid, when I stood on the high dive looking down, I was afraid, and I wasn't sure I could do it. Really, I didn't want to. Everything inside me said it was wrong. But then something happened.

My dad, seeing my fear, swam out in the pool, right where I would land. Then his voice joined in the chorus of "Jump! Jump! Jump!"

Though my father was imperfect, I knew he would catch me. I knew he wouldn't let me drown.

The situation was now different. This wasn't jumping into the unknown. This wasn't doing something I had never done. This wasn't me flailing around by myself in the deep end.

This was me jumping into my father's arms.

Suddenly I had the courage to do what I really wanted to do.

I could do that.

So can you.

I ASK GOD TO HELP ME OWN AND RELEASE MY PAST

Things have happened to us.

Things have happened because of us.

I'm not talking about good things.

I mean the bad things.

The things

we're embarrassed about,

or ashamed of.

The things

we'd rather not remember

and definitely never talk about.

There's a problem.

By trying to keep those things in the past,

we get stuck in the past,

and they block our path.

Turns out

we can't really move forward

until we own

and release

our past.

OWNING MY PAST

WHEN THE MEXICAN MAFIA shows up at your nice house in Santa Barbara threatening you and your family, you might have a problem.

Somehow Scott still didn't think he had a problem.

Scott struggled with compulsive gambling most of his life. It started with poker games in high school, then fraternity blackjack games in college. He got married and, living in Texas, didn't have many opportunities to gamble. But on each of his occasional work trips to Las Vegas, he would find himself at a blackjack table, losing all the money he had on him.

In 2002 Scott moved his family to Santa Barbara for a new job with a real estate investor. Santa Barbara was way too close to Las Vegas. Scott began making repeated trips to Sin City. His gambling addiction, mostly dormant for over a decade, went nuclear.

His first trip he lost $20,000 in one weekend. He was just getting started.

Always needing cash for gambling, Scott started borrowing from everyone he knew. He constantly lied to his wife and kids about where he was going and what he was doing. He would sit at his son's soccer game but never look up from his phone because he was frantically checking the scores of games he had bet on. He missed birthday parties because he couldn't pull himself away from the casino to get back home. All he could think about was gambling.

Soon he owed several *million* dollars to casinos in Vegas.

He owed his bookie $200,000.

He still hadn't paid back his family and friends.

The lies started catching up to him. Everything was falling apart.

Scott still couldn't see it. Despite the fallout surrounding him, he would have told you he could control his problem. He wasn't sure it even was a problem. The damage it was doing to other people? In his mind, negligible.

Victims Stay Victims

We're on a journey. This journey will change our lives.

We've realized we can't but God can. That's our step one.

So we made a decision: because we are God's children, we hand our lives over to his will. That's step two.

We're now ready for step three: I ask God to help me own and release my past.

Think of it like this: people who don't realize they're ill don't go to the doctor. If *you're* ever going to get better, you need to know you're sick. More than know it, you need to *own it*.

That means you are not a victim when it comes to your own choices.

When I talk to rehab directors, I often ask why people don't successfully rehabilitate. I get a lot of two answers. "They aren't desperate enough to want help," and "They won't own their problems."

Victims never become healthy people. Victims just stay victims.

Yes, I know, things were done to you. Yes, there were mean girls at school. Yes, your dad was inattentive. Yes, your coworker burned you. Yes, your husband walked out on you.

But even still, you made decisions. You made choices in how to respond to what happened to you and in everything else.

When it comes to your problem, whatever your problem is, you are not a victim. You cannot think of yourself as a victim. A victim mentality will never lead you toward healing or wholeness.

You need to own your past. If that's a struggle, take some time and ask God to help you answer questions like:

- Where am I to blame?
- What should I have done instead?
- How have I contributed to my problems?

In Scott's case, some friends confronted him. They told him he had a problem. They found a rehab center he could go to. After a false start, Scott got some reinforcement from his parents and sister and settled into a rehab program. He was ready to take a hard look at his life. He was ready to listen.

In rehab Scott finally owned his problems.

Let's Get Miserable!

I've been teaching the principles of recovery we're walking through in this book in one of our church's core classes for years.*

We ask people to look back at their lives and make a list of their habitual sins and the damage they've caused others. In the recovery movement, this is called taking a "moral inventory." It's the kind of self-evaluation people who want to feel clean and connected to God have been doing for thousands of years.[1]

Some people balk at the idea of reviewing their sins. Why do they have to go to that negative place? Won't this list just give them something else to hate themselves for?

---

* It might not surprise you to learn that people in Las Vegas struggle with addictions.

The point of making this list is not to discover how bad we are, and it's certainly not to make us feel worse. The point is *honesty*.

Jesus said, "The truth will set you free."[2] If we don't deal in reality, we cannot be liberated. The truth will set us free, but first it tends to make us miserable. It may not be fun, but if temporary misery is the path to long-term freedom, let's get miserable!

We can do this because we know God is not only perfect and powerful; he's also compassionate and merciful. God's unconditional love takes away the fear of acknowledging the truth about ourselves, of owning our past.

The List

We teach people in our church to make a list.

I want to ask *you* to make a list.

Take your time with it, because this can't be a superficial exercise. When something gets put on the list, it has the potential to be healed, so we want to get *everything* on the list.

Put the list in writing. Writing forces specificity. Until you put it in writing, it can still be pretty vague. Jesus said the truth will set you free, not half-truths.

It's difficult to start with a blank piece of paper, so I'll give you some categories that might help you.

One category is your *resentments*. Why? Because you might try to start thinking of what you've done but get stuck thinking about what's been done to you. So write those down as a list of resentments. People in recovery programs say, "Resentment causes violence in violent people and illness in nonviolent people." In our next step we'll talk about getting past your resentments, but for now just make a list of them. As you write them down, you may also want to put down what *you* might have done to contribute to the other person's action. (Remember, this list is about *you*.)

Another category might be your *fears*. We often sin out of fear. Maybe you were afraid that God would never provide what you wanted or that you were going to lose something you had. So perhaps list your fears and when that fear led you into a behavior that hurt people or carried you away from the life you want to live.

In rehab you also might be taught about *swollen instincts*. We all have natural instincts. Those instincts are good, but they can become bad if we let them get out of proportion or out of their proper context. Think about your natural instinct for sex, for security, for acceptance. Make a list of when those instincts have become swollen and driven you to behavior that hurt you or other people.

You also want to identify what an author named Michael Mangis calls your *signature sins*.[3] The idea is that you probably don't come up with new ways to sin. My guess is, like me, you keep going back to the same sins over and over again. Because of your past and your personality, there are certain temptations that don't appeal to you and others that pull you in like a Kardashian to a photo opportunity. So what are your signature sins? Here's a guess: there's a good chance your signature sins are related to your signature strengths. For instance, if you're a life-of-the-party extrovert, you might be prone to gossip. If you're intelligent and love to learn, you might tend to look down on others. If you're a hardworking overachiever, you might be tempted to measure success in terms of applause and recognition. If you're a peacemaker, you might shy away from confrontation when it's necessary.

It's time to own your past, so get a piece of paper and make your list.

Freedom!

Remember in the movie *Braveheart* when William Wallace yells, "Freeeeeeedooooooooom!" because he knows freedom is finally possible for the people of Scotland? Do you remember what William Wallace is doing when he yells, "Freeeeeeedoooooooom"? He's dying.

In the previous step we thought about Jesus calling us to "come and die" and how the surrender we need will feel like dying.

This step—making a list of our sins and the damage we've done, owning our past—may just add to our misery, but it's worth it because we're moving toward freedom.

My friend Scott is now free. He hasn't gambled since rehab. In fact, he was one of the inspirations for this book.* He hasn't just beaten his addiction; he is one of the wisest and most well-adjusted people I know. Think about that: the guy who owed millions to casinos and was on the hit list of the Mexican mafia is one of the wisest and most well-adjusted people I know.

Scott is free. But to become free he had to admit he wasn't free. He owned his past.

Will you?

* * *

Not sure where to even begin on your list? You're not alone. It's not an easy thing to do. Find the support of an online community of readers at TheRestoreCommunity.com. You can also download a free PDF that will help you get started on making your list.

---

* I've heard Scott say many insightful and helpful things to people. Each time I asked him, "Where did you learn that?" his answer was "Rehab." And I thought, *Man,* everyone *should go to rehab. Maybe I'll write a book about that.*

RELEASING MY PAST

I confessed to my wife over burritos. The irony was that we were in the middle of a twelve-day fast. I guess it was "Exhibit A."

I'll tell you what I confessed, but I can't quite get my nerve up yet. Give me a couple of pages.

To Be Released

We don't just want to own our past; we want God to help us *release* our past. We've been living in it, tyrannized by it, for far too long. We want it to lose its control over us. We want to be free.

We want to be free from the guilt of our past. Guilt makes us afraid and insecure. Guilt keeps us stuck in what's happened and keeps us from becoming all God wants us to be.

We want to be free from the vise grip sin has on us. And God wants us to be free too. He wants us to be released from our past so we can move into the future he has for us.

About That List

So you've made your list.

Wait, did you make your list?

No?

You've *got* to make the list.

In *Sober Mercies*, Heather Kopp tells how she was asked to make the list. She writes,

> My assignment for step one was simple. Kate asked me to write out my entire drinking history. The idea was to help me see—in case I didn't already—how unmanageable my drinking had become, and to remove any doubt in my mind that I was an alcoholic. The last thing I expected was to be surprised by my own story. But I was. Something about writing it out made the misery and the heartache of those years more real to me. I wept as I wrote about one of the greatest losses of my drinking career—something I had never before admitted to anyone. It was a baby that I never had.[1]

Heather Kopp says she was surprised by her story. When I read *Sober Mercies*, I was *shocked* by it. What shocked me wasn't that Heather was an alcoholic, or that she was a Christian and an alcoholic; it was the lengths she would go to in order to drink and to hide her drinking. She hid bottles in the boots in her closet. Once she drank those bottles, she'd put the empty ones back in her boots. A few times a week she would go up to get the dirty clothes, hide all of her empty bottles in the bottom of the laundry basket, bring them downstairs, and then secretly dispose of them in the garbage can in the garage. Her life revolved around drinking. If people were coming over, or her family was planning a trip, she would calculate how many hours it would require her to go without drinking. If it was too many, she'd probably find an excuse to cancel the plans.

It shocked me. Then it *hit* me.

I wasn't reading her book; it was reading me. I couldn't judge her, because I *was* her, not with alcohol but with food. I wanted to deny it, but I couldn't. I had to face the truth, because only the truth could set me free.

I was about to be miserable.

I made a list.

I dreaded the thought too, but you've *got* to make the list. I got out a yellow legal pad and a pen. I was on an airplane, so I constructed a wall to make sure the clown sitting next to me couldn't see what I was writing, and I put the whole embarrassing thing on paper:

Occasionally, when we have a bag of candy in the house (which, fortunately, is rare), I eat a *lot* of it. One time around Halloween I ate, like, seven consecutive peanut butter cups.

What's worse, when I threw out the wrappers, I pushed them *way* down in the garbage can, hoping no one would see them. That wasn't the first or last time I pushed the evidence of my overeating deep into the garbage.

I'm not sure when it happened, but eating has become kind of an obsession for me. When I get done with a meal or a snack, my thoughts turn to the question, "When is the next time I will eat?"

I used to eat breakfast, lunch, dinner, and (usually) a dessert. But the last several years I've been bringing small snacks to work to eat between breakfast and lunch and between lunch and dinner. It almost makes me nervous to think about going four or five hours without eating.

In the past I successfully completed fasts of up to twenty days. But the last couple of years I've cheated on my fasts. Like if I was making dinner for the family, I might eat a couple bites of what I was cooking. I justify what I'm doing with *I've got to try it and make sure it tastes good for them* and *Barely anyone fasts for as long as I do. So, yeah, I'm eating a couple of bites. But I did fast for most of the day. Who else does that?* and *Why do I have to cook their dinner anyway? Why should a person who is fasting cook dinner for other people? Of course I'm going to give in to the temptation to eat a little.*

I manipulate people to get food I want. I might say to one of the kids on the drive home from school, "You must be really hungry." When I get, "No, Dad, not really" I think, *Keep trying!* "Well, we won't have dinner for a while, so I guess I could get you something at McDonald's." "All right, Dad. I guess." *Yes!* "Well, I guess if we're gonna stop at McDonald's, I might grab something too."

Confessing the List . . . to God

I made the list.

Then I confessed it all to God. Yes, he already knew. He knew when I was living in denial. He saw me write it all down. But I still had to confess it for *me*.

That's what we do with our list. We don't write down our sins just for the sake of having a list. We write them down so we can own them and then release them. And we release them by confessing them to God and accepting his forgiveness. God promises that if we confess our sins to him, he'll forgive them.[2]

I've noticed when I confess sins to God, I'm tempted to do some things that really aren't helpful. I want to encourage you to *not* do what I'm tempted to do.

Don't *beg*. You might be tempted, like me, to beg God to forgive you. God loves you, and he *wants* to forgive you more than you want to be forgiven. He's ready and willing. You don't need to beg.

Don't *bargain*. I always find myself saying stupid things like "Please forgive me, and I promise I'll never do it again." Well, that's probably not true. So now I've added another future sin I'll need to confess to God. Stop the madness. Don't bargain. It's not necessary.

Don't *bribe*. It's easy to find yourself saying, "God, if you forgive me, I'll go to church more and give more." Again, you might not do what you're promising, and God is above your bribes anyway.

The way to confess is to *believe*. Tell God what you've done, and then choose to believe. Believe that *he is right about your sin*. The word *confess* translates the Greek word *homologea*. *Homologea* basically means to say the same thing at the same time. For so long I've been saying that what I've been doing is fine, that it's not hurting anyone. The whole time God has been saying that it isn't honoring him and that I am hurting myself and others. When I confess, I'm finally saying the same thing as God. I believe that he is right about my sin. I also believe in God's way of offering forgiveness, which is through the sacrifice his Son Jesus made for us on the cross.

When we confess like that, we become the recipients of an amazing promise God made us a long time ago: "Though your sins are like scarlet, I will make them as white as snow. Though they are red like crimson, I will make them as white as wool."[3]

That's what I wanted, so that's what I did. I made my list, and I confessed it to God. They may not have been the most insidious sins I've ever confessed, but for someone who considers himself disciplined and honest, they were some of the most embarrassing. I confessed, and I believed that I was forgiven.

That's what you need to do with your list. Remember: God is compassionate and merciful, so you can "come boldly to the throne of our gracious God."[4]

We confess to God and receive his forgiveness.

Confessing the List . . . to Another Person

We confess to God, and then we confess to another person.

God tells us it's an essential part of the recovery process: "Confess your sins to each other and pray for each other so that you may be healed."[5]

What? Why? That's awkward and humiliating and difficult! Why can't we just confess our sins to God?

Good questions. I've asked all of them myself. I'm not exactly sure why God says we need to confess to another person,* but here's my best guess.

Confessing to another person *feels more concrete.* God is more real than the other person, but because we can't see or touch him, confessing to him probably feels less real. When we confess to another person we won't later wonder whether we really confessed at all.

Confessing to another person is also *relational,* and our sins tend to be relational. Most of our sins are against people, so it makes sense that we would confess to people.

Confessing to another person *helps us know we're not alone.* Part of the power sin has over us is that it isolates us. We may feel like we're the only one who struggles like this, the only one with gross secrets like this. Then we confess to another person, and invariably that person says, in some way, "Yeah, me too." We realize the struggle is real and shared.

Confessing to another person leads to *freedom from our sin.* Again, in rehab we would learn that we're only as sick as our secrets. It's a principle we see in the Bible. Things that are hidden and kept in darkness tend to fester. When we bring something out of the darkness and into the light, it loses its power and starts to become light. So the less we hide our sin, the more we expose it, the closer we'll move to freedom from it.

So choose a friend you trust, make an appointment, and tell your friend your list. Before starting you might explain why you're doing this, that part of the path to freedom is to confess your sins to another person and have them pray for you. As you share, be honest and specific. Don't sugarcoat it or make excuses or try to justify it.

Also, don't hold back. There's going to be something you don't want to share. The secret you want to conceal the most is the one you

---

* Confessing our sins to another person is also one of the Twelve Steps. Turns out *everyone* says it's necessary.

need to reveal the most. Just confess. Then listen. Hopefully your friend will have encouraging words of love and forgiveness.

One time someone taking the "rehab" class I offer at my church asked if he could confess his sins to me. I agreed, we set up a time, and he showed up with his list. He read through it. I asked, "Did you share everything?" He hesitated and then nodded yes. I said, "Okay. I just know sometimes there's that last 5 percent we'd rather not say." He gulped. He took a deep breath. He said, "Wow, I wasn't really planning on this. This is not the way I thought this would go. Okay. Okay. I'll tell you." He then confessed his most heinous sin, something he had never told anyone. The hard man who had been stoically sitting in front of me melted. He started weeping. I asked him why. He told me it was because he was finally free.

That's what confession does. It leads to healing. It leads to freedom.

So I confessed my list to my wife. I should have confessed my list to someone immediately, but I was hesitant. My wife and I had decided to do a twelve-day fast. On the sixth day we were driving somewhere, and I brought up eating and shared some kind of justification as to why it would be all right for us to break the fast for one day and then do the rest of the days we had committed to. I was manipulating her, and it worked. As we ate our burritos, I felt sick. It wasn't the burritos. It was my sin. I had confessed it to God, but here I was, facedown in my food problem again. I was putting off confessing it to a person, partly because I was embarrassed but also because it wouldn't allow me to continue living in my sin. I felt sick because I *was* sick. I blurted out, "I have to confess something to you that I really don't want to confess to you, but I have to do it right now because I'm afraid if I don't, I never will."

I got out my list, and I confessed.

I was finally owning the food-related sins of my past. So finally I had the chance to be *released* from my past. I had the chance to be free.

How about you?

Will you own your past?

And don't you want to *release* your past? If so, you have to confess it. But will you? Will you confess it—to God and to another person?

Freedom is waiting.

Our step three: I ask God to help me own and release my past.

THE TOP TEN THINGS I, VINCE, WOULD LIKE TO CONFESS PUBLICLY TODAY

10. I have to take my shirt off when I eat spaghetti.

9. I'm tall, I have a Bigfoot costume, and my friend is a poor videographer.

8. I'm trying to start a fashion trend: sweater vests with no shirt underneath.

7. I have never shared a "sharing size" bag of M&M's.

6. I killed Colonel Mustard, in the study, with the lead pipe.

5. My arms . . . are not my real arms!

4. I shot the sheriff, but I did not shoot the deputy.

3. I was sleeping on watch duty the night my ship, the *Titanic*, hit the iceberg.

2. I thought *The Little Mermaid* was based on a true story.

1. *I* let the dogs out.

WITH GOD'S HELP, I ALWAYS FORGIVE AND ASK TO BE FORGIVEN

Remember how

"things have happened to us"

and

"things have happened because of us"—

the bad things,

so we had to own and release our past?

Guess what?

We're not done with the bad things yet.

If something bad has been done to us,

we need to forgive.

(Gulp.)

And if we've done something bad,

we need to ask for forgiveness.

(Double gulp.)

It doesn't sound fun.

But it leads to freedom.

YOU HAVE TO GO THROUGH EDOM

I HAVE NEVER watched a soap opera. I figured I didn't need to, since I lived in one.

When I was born, my family was on the run. We spent the next eleven years looking over our shoulders and making midnight escapes because of people who were after us. All those years my father never had a job. His income came from gambling, and we yo-yoed from rich to poor to rich to poor. My father was always able to win people over with his charismatic personality. This funded his gambling and also scored him some celebrity friends. I rode in limos and sat in hotel rooms with famous athletes. My dad was sometimes picked up in a helicopter that landed across the street from our house. Eventually his conning and scheming caught up to him, and he spent the rest of his life in and out of jail and even made his TV debut on *America's Most Wanted*.

When I was eleven, my mother bravely got us out of the soap opera and valiantly and successfully fought to give our family a normal life. But those first eleven years were bad. My father was angry and stressed out, and he took it out on my mother and me. He was emotionally and verbally abusive and occasionally physically abusive. It not only ruined my childhood, but it also has left a stain on me ever since.

Getting Stuck

The Bible is full of families who lived soap-opera lives. One of my favorite messed-up families, mostly because their story is so absurdly awful, features two brothers named Jacob and Esau.[1]

They were twins, with Esau coming out first. That may seem insignificant, but at that time in history the firstborn son was prized in every family. As firstborn, Esau would someday receive double the inheritance of the other children and a blessing from his father as the new leader of the family.

The story gets crazy when one day years later Esau gets hungry. Esau comes in from a long day and finds Jacob cooking lentil stew. Esau asks for a bowlful. Jacob responds, "I'll tell you what. I'll give you some stew if you give me your birthright." In other words, "You get a bowl of stew, I get half of your share of the inheritance when Dad dies." Esau says, "Well, I'm starving, so . . . okay."

How hungry would you have to be to give away half of your future inheritance for one meal? We're not talking a perfectly seared Cowboy Ribeye at Ruth's Chris with a choice of two delicious sides. No, we're talking about a bowl of lentil stew!

Esau is an idiot. *Lots* of people in the Bible are idiots. That makes me feel good because I realize I would fit right in with them. I can even relate to Esau's decision. I've never given up an inheritance for lentil stew, but I *have* traded future gifts I could have received from God for immediate gratification. Haven't we all?

- When we decided to gossip about our friend, we exchanged the blessing of a confident friendship for the immediate gratification of being able to share a juicy secret.
- When we decided to sleep with a girlfriend or boyfriend, we exchanged the blessing of purity for the immediate gratification of sexual pleasure or acceptance.
- When we decided to use our credit card to spend beyond our means, we exchanged the blessing of financial security for the immediate gratification of having more stuff.
- When we decided to yell at our spouse in anger, to make threats or throw things or punch walls, we exchanged the blessing of trusting intimacy for the immediate gratification of feeling powerful and blowing off steam.

I think we've all joined Esau in the idiot parade.

Here's the thing: when I look back at my bad decisions, it's hard not to live my life resenting myself. My life is not what it could have been, and it's my fault.

I wonder how often Esau struggled with bitterness about his own stupid decision.

Esau had traded away half his inheritance, but at least he would still receive the blessing from his father. That blessing would secure Esau's place as the leader of the family. He would be respected and honored.

But Jacob had other plans. He schemed with his mother, Rebekah, to trick his father, Isaac, into giving Esau's blessing to Jacob.

It was another blow to Esau's future, and he now had someone other than himself to blame. He could spend the rest of his life resenting himself *and* Jacob.

Again, I think we can relate. I know for me, what keeps me stuck is not only the stupid decisions I've made but also what others have done to me. I've struggled with resenting myself *and* others, especially my father.

Through Edom

Fast-forward a number of years in Jacob and Esau's story. They have both started families and both moved away from their childhood homes. Esau lives in the land of Edom. Jacob lives in a place called Paddan-aram. Esau has gathered an army of four hundred men. Jacob has gathered an army of wives and children.*

God speaks to Jacob and tells him to move back to his homeland of Canaan. Jacob rounds up his wives and kids and begins making the journey. That's when it hits him—to get to Canaan, he will have to go through Edom. Edom is where Esau and his army live. Suddenly Jacob isn't sure his caravan will be able to make it to Canaan alive.

When I read the story, my question is, Why did God want Jacob to go to Canaan? I wonder if it was because he knew Jacob and Esau could never move into the future until they addressed the past. Despite their apparent success, they must have been tormented by underlying feelings of anger, fear, and hatred. Jacob could never live the life he was supposed to live without asking Esau for forgiveness. Esau could never live the life he was supposed to live without offering Jacob forgiveness.

Jacob is terrified, and he prays, "O LORD, please rescue me from the hand of my brother, Esau. I am afraid that he is coming to attack me, along with my wives and children. But you promised me, 'I will surely treat you kindly, and I will multiply your descendants until they become as numerous as the sands along the seashore—too many to count.'"[2]

Jacob prays the kind of prayer I've prayed so many times: "God, I know I have issues from my past, but I don't want to deal with them. I just want *you* to fix them. C'mon, God. Wave your magic wand. Make it all better."

Jacob wants to get to Canaan. He wants to get to this new place God has for him. He wants to experience the blessings and promise of God. But he *doesn't* want to face his brother.

---

* We're talking about *a lot* of wives and *a lot* of children. This isn't the *Sister Wives* reality show, but it *is* a soap opera.

The problem is that life doesn't work that way. We have to go through Edom to get to Canaan. We have to get past our past to move into our future. If our relationships with people are screwed up, we're not going to be able to experience everything God has for us. In fact, those in the recovery movement have found that a person can do the first four steps (which are about getting right with God) with sincere conviction, but if they don't take the next couple of steps (which are about getting right with people), it will be just about impossible for them to maintain sobriety.

Jacob didn't want to go through Edom, but he *had* to. He had to if he was ever going to be free and if Esau was ever going to be free.

God knew that, so God sent Jacob through Edom.

When Jacob approaches Esau, he does so with a humility that reveals a truly contrite heart. Jacob owns what he has done and bows to his brother, asking for forgiveness: "As [Jacob] approached his brother, he bowed to the ground seven times before him. Then Esau ran to meet him and embraced him, threw his arms around his neck, and kissed him. And they both wept."[3]

Jacob owned what he had done and bowed to his brother, asking for forgiveness. Esau offered it, and finally they were able to move past their past and into God's future.

Our Edom

What do you need to go through in order for you to be free?

Are you committed enough to freedom to go through whatever it is?

I don't know about you, but I can tell you this: I didn't want to go to a sex-addiction group, especially since I didn't have a sex addiction, but I *had to*. I had to if I was ever going to be free.

We all want a better life for ourselves. But to get there, we have to go through Edom.

BUT WHY?

You NEED TO UNDERSTAND how hard it was raining. That's my excuse. It's why I hit the car, why I ended up looking like Mary Poppins—all of it. It's because it was raining. Hard.

We had needed a new CD player for a while, and a store was having a huge sale. So Jen and I bundled up our six-month-old son, ran out to our brand-new minivan, and drove to the store. We ran through the rain, picked out the stereo, and paid for it. I told Jen to get Dawson bundled back up, and I would bring the car around to the entrance. I got the car, pulled it around, and Jen brought Dawson out.

We now had to drive over to the purchases pickup spot. It was down a slight hill, and the quickest way was to back down it, so I glanced at the rearview mirror and put the car in reverse. As we reached the bottom of the hill there was, suddenly, a loud metallic crunch.

I assumed I had run into a pole, but when I opened my door and looked back, I realized I had hit a car: a brand-new white Mercedes-Benz. I sighed, grabbed an umbrella, and walked back to see the damage. Our back door had a large dent in it, but there was absolutely no damage to the other car. I walked back to tell my wife the news.

I noticed the owner of the car leaving the store and approaching me. He was still a long way off, but I thought he looked a lot like the rap singer Snoop Dogg. I shouted, from under my umbrella, "Hey!"

He yelled back, "You f-ing, p-ing, q-ing . . ." He was very creative with his profanity.

"You don't understand," I explained. "There's no damage to your car at all."

He screamed, "I'm gonna break your h-ing, d-ing, s-ing . . ."

"No," I said, "your car is fine."

He was now inches from me, and he reared back and took a huge swing at me but *missed*.

"Dude!" I shouted.

He pulled back and swung with all his might, aiming for my head, but *missed again*.

"Calm down, man!"

He was getting angrier by the second. He drew back, threw his fist at my face, and I felt it whiz past my ear.

Before I tell you what happened next, I'll share with you my three theories for why all of his punches missed, without my even ducking: (1) It was the man's lack of depth perception. Perhaps he wasn't wearing his glasses, or maybe he had always lived with this disability. (2) God was protecting me. Now this is the most spiritual answer and has been suggested by several of my friends who have heard this story, but it's not my best guess. No, personally I think . . . (3) It was the umbrella. Remember, as Snoop Dogg was swinging at me, I was standing there looking like Mary Poppins. The only way I could have been more Mary Poppins–like is if I had been singing, "A spoonful of sugar helps the medicine go down" in between punches. I believe that the umbrella was what threw off the man's aim. I thank God to this day for that umbrella.

So here's what happened next.

My typically mild-mannered wife rolled down the driver's side window and *screamed*, "What are you doing? People don't do this! You are hitting a minister!"

I would do *anything* to have that moment on video. I would replay it over and over again, laughing each time in hilarious delight.

So my wife stormed out her door, came around the front of the minivan, and screamed at Snoop Dogg, "I'm calling the cops!"

I gave chase, stopped her, and said, "No, you're not."

"Let's get out of here!" Snoop Dogg's friend yelled to him.

"Why not?" my wife yelled at me.

"Because of Jesus," I said.

"What does Jesus have to do with this?" my wife asked.

"Remember," I answered, "'If someone strikes you on the right cheek, turn to him the other also' and 'Love your enemies'? We don't get to pick and choose when we obey those. We forgive. We always forgive.'"*

I turned around and yelled over to Snoop Dogg, "Let's exchange insurance information."

He yelled back, "No way! You r-ing, f-ing, d-ing . . . I'm out of here!" then jumped in his car and took off.

Going to Recovery

Here's the irony: I told my wife, "We always forgive," but I wasn't actually living that way. I forgave Snoop Dogg, but I hadn't forgiven my father.

I had made a couple of halfhearted attempts to forgive him or to at least have the words "I forgive him" stumble out of my mouth, but I hadn't really forgiven him. And, as I mentioned in the introduction

---

* Yes, this all really happened, and that's really what I said. If you know me, it may be difficult to believe. Let's just say it was one of my finer moments.

to this book, that's when two of my friends told me about a recovery program for people with sex issues and addictions. I told them I didn't need a sex-addicts group. They told me that this program focused on forgiving your father. I decided to go. I had to figure out how to offer the same forgiveness to my father that I had given to Snoop Dogg.

I walked in the first night with no idea what to expect, other than feeling awkward that I'd be sitting in a circle of sex addicts without having a sex addiction myself. I soon learned that each week there was a speaker who would talk for about thirty minutes, then a ten- to fifteen-minute testimony, then an hour of small group time. I was excited to learn from the speakers how to forgive my father, until I heard the speakers. They were *horrible*. Week after week, horrible speaker after horrible speaker.* Honestly, I had to fight to stay awake.† But between periodic yet brief moments of shut-eye, those horrible speakers helped me to understand what forgiveness is and what it isn't.

What Forgiveness Isn't

I learned that *forgiveness is not forgetting*. People love to say, "forgive and forget," but we *can't* erase memories. We don't work like that. If we try to forget without forgiving, all we're doing is submerging our feelings. It's like a beach ball held under water in a swimming pool. The feelings are still there, just under the surface, pushing their way to the top, and eventually they *will* pop back up. Forgiveness is *not* forgetting.

I also discovered that *forgiveness is not waiting*. We've all heard the saying, "Time heals all wounds." Uh, no, it *doesn't*. Forgiveness isn't waiting for the pain to stop or waiting for the other person to say, "I'm sorry." The Bible tells us, "As far as it depends on you, live at peace with everyone."[1] I realized I had a responsibility to take the initiative and offer forgiveness.

---

* I will admit that I'm a bit of a speaker snob. I think Martin Luther King Jr.'s "I Have a Dream" speech could have used a few more rhymes, and Abe Lincoln should have started the Gettysburg Address with a couple of jokes to warm up the crowd.

† Super honestly, I would bring a bag of M&M's each week and eat them as slowly as I could while the speaker talked. I did this based on my belief that you can't fall asleep while eating. That belief was severely tested.

I also learned that *forgiveness is not pretending nothing happened.* Horrible speaker number nineteen (this was a twenty-six-week recovery program) talked about how we've all experienced having a fight with someone that led to hurt feelings and a fractured relationship. Then somehow, inexplicably, one day, everything was cool again. We acted like nothing had happened and didn't discuss the situation. We avoided a confrontation, but that is *not* forgiveness. When God says we are to forgive, he's not talking about sweeping the problem under the rug.

Perhaps most important, I learned that *forgiving someone doesn't mean that what they did was okay.* Horrible speaker number twenty-two showed us a Bible verse: "Do not repay anyone evil for evil."[2] God calls what was done to us evil. And I realized, God forgave *me.* When he forgave me, he wasn't saying what I did was okay. No, it's sin. This was critical for me to understand. I knew what was done to me was evil, and I had always felt like forgiving would be like saying it wasn't. But, no, it *was* evil. Even still, God was telling me to forgive it.

What Forgiveness Is

As I kept myself hyped on caffeine and slowly ate candy, I listened to the speakers and the testimonies, participated in the small group discussions, and began not only to move past my misconceptions of what forgiveness *isn't* but to get a grasp on what forgiveness *is.*

Forgiveness is releasing my hope for a better past. Much of our inability to forgive stems from thinking about what could (and should) have been. But I realized part of forgiveness is finally accepting what really happened. I can't change that. I wish I could, but I can't. I'll never be able to. So I need to release my hope for a better past. The past I got is the past I have.

We need to release our hope for a better past not only because we can't change the past, but also because if we continue to hold on to bitterness about what happened, it can ruin our *future.*

When we forgive, it doesn't change our *past*, but it can change our *path*. What *happened* doesn't change, but what *can happen* does.

Forgiveness is also releasing my right to retaliate. When I release my past, I'm finally able to do that. I found out the word *forgive* is actually a financial term. It means "to cancel a debt." The heart of anger says, "You owe me." When you've been hurt, you feel like that person owes you something.

- If you grew up in a broken home, someone robbed you of the opportunity to be tucked in by both a mom and dad who love you.
- If your spouse left you, you were robbed of the kind of marriage you were promised at the altar.
- If you were double-crossed in a business deal, someone took money and opportunity from you.

When we carry our anger, we keep the account open until the person repays us. But the problem is people can't repay most of the things they owe us. How can you be paid back a childhood? How can you be paid back a marriage? So we carry around this debt without any hope of repayment, and that frustration leads us to seek to repay people for what they did to us. But in forgiveness we give up our right to seek revenge, to "repay anyone evil for evil."

Retaliation is the natural rhythm of our world, but Jesus calls us to something different and better. He taught, "You have heard that it was said, 'Eye for eye, and tooth for tooth.' But I tell you, do not resist an evil person. If anyone slaps you on the right cheek, turn to them the other cheek also."[3]

That's really difficult. It's unnatural. It's also unfair.

But still, it is what God asks us to do. It's what he tells *all of us* to do.

During the days of apartheid, a South African policeman named van de Broek and some fellow officers showed up at the home of a poor black family. They took the eighteen-year-old son out in the yard and, in front of the mother and father, burned the boy to death. Eight years later van de Broek and some policemen returned to the same home. They forced the wife to watch as they poured gasoline over her husband's body and burned him to death as well.[4]

This woman had now witnessed the deaths of her son and her husband by the same evil men and would have to live the rest of her life with those memories—and without her husband and son.

That woman happened to be a Christian. Because she was a Christian, she was expected to forgive.

For her to forgive would not be natural.

It would not be fair.

But still, it *was* what God was telling her to do.

It was also what God was telling *me* to do.

But Why?

Thanks to the DRED Talks,* I finally understood forgiveness. It was releasing my hope for a better past and releasing my right to retaliate. I knew what God wanted me to do, but I still didn't understand why. *Why* was God asking me to forgive my father?

I thought, *He doesn't deserve it. He doesn't care. He didn't apologize.*

But as I progressed through the recovery program, I finally had an epiphany. Offering my father forgiveness wasn't about *he*. It was about *me*.

Forgiving may not heal the other person. But when we forgive, we heal ourselves.

I read a story about Nelson Mandela, who unjustly spent twenty-seven grueling years in prison. Four years after his release, he was inaugurated as president of South Africa, and he invited one of the abusive prison guards to be there with him for his special moment. He reconciled with the white government who had wrongly kept him in jail all those years. He invited Percy Yutar to have dinner with

---

* Do you see what I did there? You've heard of the TED Talks—great speakers giving speeches on important topics. My recovery program featured the "DRED" Talks—get it?

him. Yutar was the state prosecutor at the trial in which Mandela was convicted of sabotage and sentenced to hard labor for life. Yutar had demanded the death penalty for Mandela.

Later, Bill Clinton asked Mandela why. Why did he forgive all those people? Mandela explained that all those people had controlled him for twenty-seven years. When he got out of jail, he didn't want them to continue controlling his life. He told Clinton, "You simply cannot be free without forgiveness."[5]

I finally came to understand that not forgiving my father wasn't hurting *him*. It was hurting *me*. Forgiving him probably wouldn't set him free, but it *would* set me free.

I realized I had to do it. I had to forgive my father.

But How?

The question then became, How? *How* could I forgive him?

I'll tell you in the next chapter how I finally answered that question, but first I want to make this personal for you: Whom do you need to forgive?

I learned in sex rehab that when you trace addiction back, it often grows out of the soil of unforgiveness. Forgiveness is the key that will unlock the prison door and get you out of the cell you've been stuck in.

So, whom do you need to forgive?

THE TOP TEN SIGNS YOU NEED TO FORGIVE

10. In high school you were voted "Most Likely to Get Even."

9. Under "hobbies" you always write, "carrying grudges."

8. You no longer say hello to the diabetic neighbor who didn't have a cup of sugar to give you.

7. You refuse to play the board game Sorry.

6. Your dog's name is Vengeance.

5. You haven't spoken in days because everyone in your life is receiving the silent treatment.

4. You think road rage gets a bad rap.

3. You've got 99 problems, and people are *all* of them.

2. You've got a Google Doc titled "People's houses I plan to egg this year."

1. Because of this top ten list, you want to punch me in the throat.

BUT HOW?

Louis Zamperini grew up in the 1920s in Torrance, California. He was a troubled kid but discovered he could run fast. In fact, he became a track star in the Berlin Olympics.

He enlisted in the Army Air Corps, knowing he'd see action in World War II. In May 1943, the plane he was in lost two of its engines and crashed into the middle of the Pacific Ocean. Instantly eight of the eleven men were killed.

The three who survived, including Louis, had two lifeboats, no water, and no food. They survived on rainwater and raw fish. They were shot at by Japanese planes, and sharks circled their rafts regularly. After thirty-three days one of the men died.

After forty-seven days lost at sea, they washed ashore in the Marshall Islands and were immediately captured by the Japanese.

Louis became a prisoner of war. Japan was the last place you wanted to be a POW. During the war, one percent of the prisoners in German and Italian POW camps died. In Japanese POW camps, 37 percent of the POWs died due to the brutal treatment they received.

Louis was first taken to what was nicknamed "Execution Island." He found the names of nine marines carved into the ceiling of his cell and learned they had all been beheaded with a samurai sword. He added his name to the list, assuming he wouldn't live to tell his tale.

When his Japanese captors weren't beating him or forcing him into hard labor, they used him as a test subject for horrible medical experiments.

Later he was transferred to a different POW camp under the command of Sergeant Mutsuhiro Watanabe. Watanabe tortured his prisoners with beatings and degrading acts, forcing them to do push-ups in human waste and to lick his boots.

Watanabe had a special disdain for Louis.

He beat him across the face with the metal end of his belt. At one point he lined up the prisoners and instructed them to each punch Louis as hard as they could. Those who didn't would be subject to execution. Louis passed out from the beating and couldn't walk for days.

After several months of relentless abuse, one day an American airplane appeared on the horizon, flashing red lights in Morse code: "The war is over!"

Louis was eventually brought back home. He met his family at an airport in America in September 1945.

You would think Louis's trials were over, but they weren't. They followed him home. Every night as he slept, he relived his excruciating torture as Watanabe showed up in his dreams.

He turned to alcohol, hoping to prevent the nightmares by drinking himself to sleep every night.

One night his dream was different—he was able to grab hold of his torturer, and he began to choke him, hoping to kill him, enjoying listening to his screams. Then he woke up and realized he had been choking his wife. The screams were hers.

She told him divorce was inevitable, and Louis's life became even darker. Life around him was going on as normal, but he was still stuck in Japan.

Louis came up with a plan. He concluded the only way to escape his ongoing mental torture was to return to Japan to find, and to kill, his Japanese tormentor.

Us

I can't compare what I went through to the torture Louis Zamperini experienced, but I was dealing with something that was incredibly hard to forgive. My father, one of only two people in the world obligated to make me feel loved, had made me feel unlovable.

I was finally getting to a place where I understood why I should forgive him, and I truly wanted to forgive him, but how could I do it?

I read the Bible, and it made it sound so easy. For instance, "Get rid of all bitterness, rage and anger, brawling and slander, along with every form of malice. Be kind and compassionate to one another, forgiving each other, just as in Christ God forgave you."[1]

It's like, "You're bitter? You have unforgiveness in your life? Well, get rid of it."

I read that and wanted to argue, "But you don't understand what happened to me. Let me tell you my story . . ." It's like God's response was, "Okay, yes, you have a story. But still, get rid of it."

I knew it made sense. If I went to a doctor and he told me I had cancer, my issue would not be how I got it but how to get rid of it. But for some reason, with an issue of the heart, I don't want to know how to get rid of it; I want to talk about how I got it. I realize that may be understandable, but it's also *crazy*, because unforgiveness is a cancer, and no matter how I got it, I needed to get rid of it.

I *wanted* to get rid of it, but I was incapacitated by not understanding *how* to get rid of it. Then the horrible speakers and awkward discussions from my recovery program came to my rescue. I think I can break down what I learned into three steps.*

Learning How to Forgive

Step 1: Acknowledge your sin and realize that God has offered to forgive you. It seems we have to start by realizing we are forgiven—"forgiv[e] each other, just as in Christ God forgave you."[2]

Like you, I had a story. I used my story to justify why I couldn't possibly forgive. The sin against me was too great, the wound I suffered too deep to just get rid of it. But what helped me was to look in the mirror and ask, *Is the story of what happened to me worse than what happened to Jesus?*

I thought about Jesus' story: God created us in love. We disobeyed God and spit in God's face. We deserved death. So God sent his Son Jesus in love to rescue us from our sin. Jesus went around loving people, teaching people, and healing people. In return, Jesus was wrongfully accused, beaten, whipped, and nailed naked to a cross, all for crimes he never committed, and he took on the sin of the world, thus separating himself from the perfect intimacy he had experienced for all eternity past with his Father.

Is my story worse than that? No. Is yours?

What we deserve is for God to carry out his wrath against us. Instead, God offers to forgive us.

The more I looked at it that way, the more difficult it became to justify my unwillingness to forgive my father. I realized the way to forgive him was "just as in Christ God forgave you." That's the first step.

Step 2: Actually be forgiven by reaching out for God's forgiveness. Just because someone offers you a present doesn't mean you have the present. You need to accept it, to reach out and take it from their hands so it's now in your possession. Just because God has offered to forgive

---

* Wouldn't it be nice if life were really that easy? "You can do this in three simple steps!" Well, I'm not saying these steps are simple or easy, but they do lay out the path of *how* to forgive.

you doesn't mean you've received his forgiveness. To actually be for-given, you need to say yes, to reach out and receive it.

One of the horrible speakers pointed out that if you haven't received forgiveness, how can you give it? You can't give away some-thing you don't have.

I thought of it this way. If I asked you to give away a million dol-lars, you couldn't, because you don't *have* a million dollars. If I asked you to give away a Lamborghini, you couldn't, because you don't *have* a Lamborghini.[†]

You can't give away something you don't have. If you haven't *received* forgiveness, I'm not sure you can *give* forgiveness.

Once you say yes and receive God's forgiveness, it changes you.

That's what happened with Louis Zamperini. Remember how he decided to go back to Japan and kill the man who tortured him?

Before he could do that, his wife told him she was going to hear a speaker and wanted him to come with her. He did. The speaker's name was Billy Graham, and he talked about God's offer of forgive-ness through Jesus. Louis said yes to God's offer. He surrendered the whole broken mess of his life to God. He asked God to forgive him for his sins. And God did. God not only forgave him, God eventually *healed* him. The love and forgiveness of God changed him. Louis's heart was filled up with the love and forgiveness of God.

Finally he had forgiveness, so he finally had forgiveness to give away.

That's what he did.

He went back to Japan, visited many of the guards from his POW days, and let them know he had forgiven them.[‡]

Many of the war criminals who had committed the worst atroci-ties were held in a prison in Tokyo. In 1950 Louis went and spoke

---

[†] Unless you *do* have a Lamborghini, in which case, I *am* asking you to give away your Lamborghini . . . to me! And if you do have a million dollars, you can put that in the trunk before you give it to me!

[‡] By the way, if you watch the movie about Zamperini's life, *Unbroken*, it does not give an accurate chronology. We learn that Louis offered his tormentors forgiveness and *then* see (after the final scene of the movie) that he embraced God's forgiveness. But if you read the books about him (*Devil at My Heels* or *Unbroken*), you'll see that Louis said it was only because of first receiving God's forgiveness that he was able to offer it to others.

to those prisoners, sharing how his life had been changed through God's forgiveness and how God was now offering that same forgiveness to them.

The man in charge of the prison encouraged any of the prisoners who recognized Zamperini because they had him as a POW to come forward and meet him. Louis embraced each one and offered them forgiveness.[*]

When you say yes and receive God's forgiveness, it changes you.

The trick, it seems, is to make sure it does, and to make sure you *stay* changed. That leads right into step 3. Step 3 was the part I had been struggling with.

Step 3: Always remain in the role of one who needs forgiveness, never taking the role of judge.

When my kids Dawson and Marissa were young, I wanted to help them understand God's offer of forgiveness and that Jesus had to suffer so we could be forgiven. So I made a family policy: if one of them did something wrong and deserved a spanking,[†] the other (innocent) child could elect to take the spanking in the guilty one's place. I explained to them that this is what Jesus did for us. We were guilty; he was innocent. But he chose to "take our spanking."

They seemed to understand, but no one got in trouble for a while, so we never had a chance to test out my new system. Finally we were driving somewhere and the kids were acting up, especially Marissa. I gave a warning or two. Then I realized it might be a good chance to remind them of our family's spanking policy. So I explained if Marissa kept up her bad behavior and it warranted a spanking, Dawson could choose to take the spanking for her. It got quiet in the car for a couple of minutes, and then Marissa started whining. I asked why, and she said, "Daddy, when do I get to spank Dawson? I want to spank Dawson!"

---

[*] He attempted to meet with Watanabe, his most brutal tormentor, so he could offer forgiveness to him, but Watanabe refused.

[†] If you promise not to judge me for being a parent who spanks, I promise not to judge you for being a parent who doesn't.

Marissa was given a chance to avoid a punishment she deserved, and instead of being grateful, all she wanted was to dole out punishment to someone else! The problem with Marissa was that she wasn't viewing herself as being guilty and in need of forgiveness but instead had put herself in the role of judge.

That was my problem too. The reason I found it so difficult to forgive my father was because I was playing judge, quick to determine guilt and assign penalties, rather than viewing myself as one in need of forgiveness.

Maybe that has been your problem too.

Did you ever read about Mark Morice? Just after Hurricane Katrina hit New Orleans, Mark saw flood victims hanging on to rooftops and clinging to tree branches. He realized these people were going to die. Then he noticed an eighteen-foot pleasure boat. He didn't know it, but the boat belonged to a man named John Lyons. Morice isn't the kind of guy who steals, but this was a desperate moment and called for desperate measures. Driven by compassion, Morice took the boat and rescued over two hundred people with it. Later he passed the boat on to others who used it to rescue more people. Ultimately the boat was lost. After all the chaos, John Lyons, the boat's owner, was looking for the boat, and Morice identified himself, explaining that he took the boat and saved hundreds of people in it. John Lyons sued Mark Morice for $12,000.

Why? Partially because insurance wouldn't cover the full cost of the boat. But really, because Lyons took the role of judge rather than viewing himself as someone in need of mercy. Think about it. If Mark Morice had saved John Lyons that day, or had saved one of John Lyons's kids, there wouldn't have been a lawsuit. Why not? Because John Lyons would have seen himself as someone in need of mercy.[3]

I realized that my trouble forgiving my father stemmed from being more focused on someone else's need for punishment than on being grateful for my being forgiven.

How could I forgive my father? The first step was to acknowledge my sin and realize that God had offered to forgive me. Second was to actually be forgiven by reaching out for God's forgiveness. The third step, the most difficult one for me, was to always remain in the role of one who needs forgiveness instead of jumping out of the mercy seat and into the judge's chair.

The Decision—With, and Without, Feeling

I made the decision to forgive my father.

One thing that had tripped me up on my journey toward forgiveness was waiting for the right emotions. I assumed I needed to *feel* forgiving. But horrible speaker number twenty-five helped me understand that in the same way I want my daughter to clean her room even if she doesn't "feel like it," I needed to obey God even if the emotions weren't there. I finally understood that forgiving is an action, not a feeling. If I waited for the emotion, I would wait forever. I also learned that while we like to wait for feelings to motivate us to take action, the truth is that feelings tend to *follow* our actions. So I made the decision. Without emotion, without feeling like I wanted to, I made the decision to forgive my father.

And I did.

But I still wanted my feelings to match up—to match up with God's gracious feelings toward me and with the action I had now taken. I didn't want my forgiveness to seem incomplete, and I didn't want bitter feelings returning or taking root in my life. I wanted to develop forgiving feelings, emotions of love and compassion for my father, which I don't think I had ever experienced for him.

I knew I couldn't do it. So I did what I *could* do. I prayed. I asked God for help. That's when I learned a third aspect of what forgiveness is. Remember how I had learned that forgiveness is releasing my hope for a better past and releasing my right to retaliate? There's one more piece.

Forgiveness is *releasing the power of Jesus into my life.*

Remember step 1: "I can't; God can."

I wondered if my previous attempts to forgive my father hadn't worked because I had attempted to forgive him in my own power.

God understands our limitations. He knows this is difficult, so he doesn't ask me to do it on my own. God offers to help me live the life he's asking me to live.

I knew I needed that.

I couldn't imagine having forgiving feelings toward my father, but I knew God had the power to do unimaginable things.

After being released from prison, Nelson Mandela told the black people of his country that there were white people who deserved justice, but there was no time for justice. Instead, what was needed was reconciliation. To move past revenge and toward forgiveness, Mandela set up the Truth and Reconciliation Commission. Archbishop Desmond Tutu was appointed to head up this official government institution, which acted much like a court of law but with a significant twist. If a white police or army officer confessed his crimes in front of the commission and his victims and their family members, honestly sharing the brutalities he had committed against them, and then apologized, he would not be prosecuted for those crimes.

It was quite controversial. Many black South Africans felt it unfair that these men could escape justice, but Mandela insisted that healing was more essential for the country to move forward.

One of the men who went before the Truth and Reconciliation Commission to confess his crimes was Officer van de Broek. Remember him? In front of the woman who was mother to the eighteen-year-old boy and wife to the man he had killed, Officer van de Broek shared all the gory details of what he had done.

When finished, the judge asked this now elderly woman, "What do you want from Mr. van de Broek?"

She said, "Mr. van de Broek took all my family away from me, and I still have a lot of love to give. Twice a month, I would like for him to come to the ghetto and spend a day with me so I can be a mother to him. And I would like Mr. van de Broek to know that he is forgiven by God, and that I forgive him too. I would like to embrace him so he can know my forgiveness is real."[4]

A stunned silence came over the courtroom. Finally it was broken by a solitary voice. At the back of the room someone started singing an old song, written by a slave trader two hundred years earlier who knew all about being forgiven: "Amazing grace, how sweet the sound, that saved a wretch like me." Everyone in the courtroom was deeply moved, except for Officer van de Broek. He was unconscious. Fainting was his response to being forgiven and the offer of embrace. He was literally knocked unconscious by grace.

Wow.

So I prayed, knowing that God is completely capable of doing what seems unimaginable in people.

Forgiving and loving my father was unfair and unnatural, so I asked God to do it in a *super*natural way in me.

I can't. God can.

God did.

One day, it happened. Something snapped. Supernaturally snapped. After a long journey, not only did I decide to take the action of forgiving my father, I actually *felt* forgiving toward him. I wondered what had led him to the life he was living. I hoped somehow he would end up in heaven.

Finally, I really experienced forgiveness. I experienced forgiveness for my father, and I felt free.* In a deeper way than I ever had before, I experienced God's forgiveness for me. All of it changed my life in so many ways.

You

I want to tell you: if I can, you can. If I can forgive, you can forgive.

Well, let me say that in a different way.

---

* My father had died several years earlier, so unfortunately I was not able to tell him I forgave him. But that's an important point: if forgiveness were just about and for my father, once he died, I wouldn't have had to still forgive him. But forgiveness was much more about and for me, so I still had to. You may not be able to forgive someone to his or her face, but you still need to forgive that person for your sake.

I can't. God can. God did in me.

If God can in me, God can in you.

It may be a journey for you like it's been for me. I don't know.

But I do know this: you have to forgive.

If you care about what God says in the Bible, you have to do it because he says so. But even if you don't care, you have to do it because you care about you. You'll never get unstuck without forgiveness. If you want to be free, you have to forgive. But you don't have to do it on your own.

Step 4: With God's help, I always forgive and ask to be forgiven.

BUT WHAT ABOUT ME?

RICH WAS AT A CROSSROADS, a dividing line that would set the course for the rest of his life. It was all about forgiveness, but not the type you might think.

I met Rich at the grand opening of a church I started in Virginia Beach back in 1998. We became friends and ended up in a men's group together. Soon it came out that Rich was in the middle of an affair with a woman from work. Rich painfully confessed the affair to us, then to God, then to his wife.

Rich accepted God's promise of forgiveness.

Rich's wife forgave him, and he gratefully accepted her forgiveness. Then Rich got stuck.

Rich could not forgive himself. God and his wife had shown him grace, but he didn't have any for himself. That was his crossroads. Would he forgive himself?

Maybe You . . .

A few years after I learned about forgiving others, I did a teaching series on it at my church that seemed to help a lot of people. What was interesting was that the person most of our people struggled to forgive was themselves.

Maybe you can relate. Maybe you . . .

- physically hurt someone in some way
- wrecked your marriage
- weren't there for your kids
- were involved in an accident that seriously injured someone
- had an abortion when you were younger
- had an affair
- went through a rebellious period in your teens, and it really damaged your parents
- were in the military and can't forget what you saw and did
- ruined someone financially in a shady business deal

You may wonder, *How do I forgive myself? What do I have to do to feel forgiven?*

Two Types of Guilt

One thing that has helped me is distinguishing between two types of guilt, what some call "true guilt" and "phantom guilt."

True guilt comes from something you *should* feel guilty about. Guilt is not necessarily a bad thing. When we sin against God or other people, guilt is the proper response. It's a *helpful* response, because that feeling of conviction is intended to change our behavior and lead us to ask God for forgiveness and to make amends.

When we ask God to forgive us, he does. The Bible says, "If we confess our sins, he is faithful and just and will forgive us our sins and purify us from all unrighteousness."[1] In fact, the Bible tells us God stops remembering our sin. God says, "Their sins . . . I will remember no more."[2] *We* can't forget, but apparently God can.

At that point, our guilt has served its purpose and is no longer necessary. If we continue to feel guilty about something we've confessed and been forgiven for, that's phantom guilt.

Phantom guilt happens because of the way our brains and emotions work. Just because we've been forgiven doesn't mean the memory of what we've done has been deleted. So we get confused, assuming that because we can remember it, God remembers it as well.

What's worse is that we not only remember the sin we've committed but also the guilty feelings that go along with the memory. But those feelings of guilt are phantoms. They exist in our minds, so they *feel* real, but they don't exist in the mind of God. When we asked for forgiveness, God forgave us and completely forgot what we did. In his mind it no longer exists. The problem is that it's still very real to us. It's phantom guilt.

But Why and But How?: Yourself

I think it'd be helpful to remember what forgiveness isn't, what it is, and how we can give forgiveness, this time applying it to ourselves.

Forgiveness is not saying it wasn't wrong. Part of the reason we won't forgive ourselves is because we know what we did was wrong. Yeah, it was. But you still need to forgive yourself. When you do, you're *not* saying it wasn't wrong.

Forgiveness is not forgetting. We can't forget what we've done. Honestly, we'll never forget. But we still need to, and can, forgive ourselves.

Forgiveness is not pretending it didn't happen. We may not want to forgive someone because we think it means we're letting that person get away with it. The same issue may trip us up when it comes to forgiving ourselves. I know I deserve to be punished, so I won't let myself off the hook by letting go of my guilt. But forgiveness is not pretending it didn't happen. Forgiveness is not ignoring sin; it's dealing with sin in love.

We've learned what forgiveness is not, and also what it *is*.

Forgiveness is releasing my hope for a better past. We can't change the past, and if we continue to live in it, it can ruin our future. When we forgive ourselves, it doesn't change our *past*, but it can change our *path*. You have a God who loves you and is saying, "You've beaten yourself up enough." God wants you to move on and is offering you the gift of a better future. When you say, "I know God has forgiven me, but I can't forgive myself," you're refusing to accept God's gift of a better future.

Forgiveness is also releasing my right to retaliate. Jesus taught, "You have heard the law that says, 'Love your neighbor' and hate your enemy. But I say, love your enemies!"[3] What if you are your own worst enemy? Do you get to exclude yourself from loving your enemies?

But maybe you did something evil. God tells us, "Do not repay anyone evil for evil."[4] You have to stop thinking evil thoughts about yourself because of what you've done.

Forgiveness also releases the power of Jesus into my life. You need to forgive yourself. God knows it's not easy, so if you look to him as you obey him, he will empower you to do what you need to do.

We've also learned *why* God tells us to forgive.

God doesn't want me to forgive to heal the other person but to heal *me*. You need to forgive you to heal *you*.

This can be difficult because usually another person was hurt by our actions. When I forgive someone for what they did to me, it makes sense because I'm the offended party. But it can be hard to forgive myself because I offended someone else. So I may feel like, *I'm not the one to forgive myself. That person needs to forgive me.* Part of the process of forgiving myself will involve going to the person I've wronged to apologize and try to make amends.

But whether someone accepts an apology or not, you still need to forgive yourself. Remember, forgiving yourself is not saying it wasn't wrong. The person you apologize to and ask forgiveness from may say, "No, because what you did was wrong!" Yes, it was. But that person still has the option to forgive you, and you still need to forgive yourself. When you do, you're not saying it wasn't wrong.

We've also learned *how* we can forgive.

You first need to realize that God has offered to forgive you, even though your sins were responsible for the death of his Son Jesus.

Then you need to actually be forgiven. It's not popular to say this in our day, but not everyone is forgiven by God. God offers forgiveness to everyone, but you only receive it if you say yes. You embrace God's forgiveness by putting your faith in Jesus and what he did for you on the cross.

Once you have God's forgiveness, you have it to give. You can't give what you don't have. Once you receive it, you can offer it to others *and* to yourself.

Who Pays for Forgiveness?

So you can forgive yourself. Or can you?

I'll sound like I'm contradicting myself, but there's a sense in which you can't forgive yourself. Why? Because real forgiveness always involves a cost.

Pastor Tim Keller uses this illustration. Let's say I go to your house and, pulling in to your driveway, knock over your mailbox. Someone has to pay for a new mailbox.

If you *don't* forgive me, *I'll* pay for it.

If you *do* forgive me, *you'll* pay for it.

But either way, *someone* has to pay for a new mailbox.

Real forgiveness *always* involves a cost.

Let's say someone cheats you out of money in a shady business deal. You can choose not to forgive them, and they still owe you the money. Or you can choose to forgive them; then you have to eat the cost. *Someone* has to pay the lost money.

We may not think of it this way, but there is always a cost to sin. I've sinned, and there are consequences, so someone has to pay. You've sinned, and someone has to pay. The reason God is able to offer you forgiveness is because Jesus has already paid the penalty of your sin on the cross.

That's why it is true in a sense that we can't truly forgive ourselves, because we can't pay the cost for what we've done.

We can feel guilty about it, we can beat ourselves up about it, but we can't pay the cost.

Right?

Let's say you hurt someone by manipulating the relationship and taking advantage of the person. You have guilt because of what you've done. The two options of resolution would be that you *don't* forgive yourself and you bear the guilt. Or you *do* forgive yourself but you *still* bear the guilt.

Either way, you're stuck with the guilt.

Some people* would say, "Just let it go." That sounds nice,† but what does it really mean? Pretend it didn't happen? But it did. Act like it wasn't a big deal? But it was.

You can't pay the cost of your sin, so you continue to bear the guilt of your sin. What we need is someone who can say, "I will pay the cost *and* I will bear the guilt." That's why we need Jesus. He's the only one who has ever offered to pay the cost and bear the guilt for us.

You can't really forgive yourself for what you've done, but God can forgive you. Once God has forgiven you, Jesus takes the cost and the guilt of your sin,‡ and now that you've been given forgiveness, you have forgiveness to give. So once God has forgiven you, you *can* forgive yourself.

Held Captive by Lies or Set Free by Truth?

All of this should make you feel free. You don't have to beat yourself up over your sin anymore.

In fact, think about what you're really saying when you do beat yourself up for what's already been forgiven. It's like you're saying,

---

* And Disney princesses.
† Especially when sung by a Disney princess.
‡ The Bible says it this way: "Therefore, there is now no condemnation for those who are in Christ Jesus" (Romans 8:1, NIV).

"I know you're God, but I have higher standards than you do. You may think Jesus' death was enough, but I don't think so. You may think my sin and condemnation have been removed, but I don't think so."

When we refuse to forgive ourselves, we're insulting God.

When we refuse to forgive ourselves, we're basing our lives on lies. You may think you've ruined your life, you're irreparably broken, and there's no future for you, but those are lies. The truth sets you free, and the truth is that you are not defined by your sin but by God's love. The truth is that God still has a plan for your life. In fact, God can even use your mistakes to accomplish his purposes. In God's economy, nothing is ever wasted, including our sin and pain.[§]

That brings me back to my friend Rich.

Remember that he ended his affair, confessed to God and his wife, and accepted their forgiveness. The issue was forgiving *himself*. He couldn't imagine how he could ever look himself in the mirror or how God could ever use him for good.

He struggled but eventually realized that if God forgave him, who was he not to forgive himself? Because God had forgiven him, he could forgive himself.

So he did, and something changed.

God's love flooded into his heart. He became one of the most loving people I knew—to his wife and to everyone else.

He really grew in his faith and eventually into leadership roles in our church.

He decided he wanted to serve God full time. He went back to college and got a degree in ministry.

He ended up starting a church in his hometown of Philadelphia. He saw lots of lives changed there.

One of the cool things at our church in Virginia and the church he started in Philadelphia was that he and his wife were able to help so many couples with struggling marriages. Why? Well, they had been

---

§ The Bible tells us, "We know that in all things God works for the good of those who love him, who have been called according to his purpose" (Romans 8:28, NIV).

through it. Rich's affair didn't disqualify him from ministry; it set him up for ministry.

Rich later got brain cancer, and he died a couple of years ago. He had touched so many lives that the family had to have multiple funerals in different cities.

I just can't help but think, What if Rich had never accepted God's forgiveness? What if he had never forgiven himself? What if he had continued to think he had ruined his life and had no future? He would have lived out his days in a prison of regret. Instead, he lived out his days in the freedom of grace, impacting countless lives by sharing that grace with others.

What about you?

Are you the hardest person for you to forgive?

Do you feel like you've blown it and your life can never be quite the same?

That's a lie.

Your sin does not define you.

God's love is bigger than your worst mistake.

Jesus paid the cost and took the guilt of your sin.

There is no condemnation left for you.

God still has a great plan for your life.

It's time to stop hating the enemy you've made yourself into.

It's time to stop repaying yourself evil for evil.

It's time to forgive yourself so that you can be free.

TIME TO GET EVEN

I HAVE A CONFESSION TO MAKE. I put headphones on when I get dropped off at the airport and don't take them off until I leave the next airport. I do this so no one will talk to me. I realize that doesn't fit the whole "love your neighbor" concept super well, but I've got my reasons.*

One time I was sitting at an airport gate, wearing my headphones, getting some work done before boarding the flight. That's when I heard it. "It" was a seemingly loud noise. I thought it odd that I could hear anything, since I have noise-canceling headphones, but I chose to ignore it.

Then I heard it again. It almost sounded like words, like hearing a radio DJ through a lot of static. I looked up, and it seemed like

---

* You might call my reasons "excuses." What are they? (1) I'm an introvert. (2) I have lots of work to do. (3) Um. I like music. (4) Um. I look good in headphones? (5) Did I mention I'm an introvert?

people were looking at me. *That's weird,* I thought. But, again, I chose to ignore it.

Then it happened again. I heard a loud metallic, almost Charlie Brown's–teacher kind of voice. I looked up. People were not only looking in my direction; they were laughing.

I thought, *Oh no, whatever it is, it's me.* My best guess was that my headphones were malfunctioning, somehow projecting distorted sound that everyone else was hearing. So I very carefully, trying to mitigate whatever embarrassment was about to hit me, took off my headphones.

When I did, I heard it again. This time, though, it was much clearer. "Herb! Where are you? Herb? Do you hear me?" Startled, I looked to my right and I saw him. Herb. Herb was an old airport security guard, and he was sound asleep in the chair next to me. He was snoring a little, but the sound I heard wasn't that. It was his walkie-talkie. The voice came through it again, "Herb? You are not where you are supposed to be. Herb! We need you at the security check for the A and B gates. Herb, where are you?"

I thought about waking Herb up. He was clearly in the wrong place, doing the wrong thing. But before I could make a decision, Herb woke up all on his own, stretched, stood up, and walked away. Everyone at the gate seemed very happy for Herb. I was just happy they hadn't been laughing at me.

Wrong Place, Wrong Thing

I'll get back to Herb, but first I need to vent about something.

As a pastor, part of my job is to stand on a stage every week and give a message. Not much drives me crazier than when people get up during the message and walk out. They always come back, so I realize they just needed a break to go to the restroom or to make a phone call, but I'm not hearing those excuses. When we're at church and someone walks out, I always want to say, "Excuse me. Are you in the wrong place? Are you doing the wrong thing? I mean, seriously, is there *ever* a good reason to walk out on worshiping God?"

Turns out there *is*.

One time Jesus was teaching and he said, "If you are offering your gift at the altar and there remember that your brother or sister has something against you, leave your gift there in front of the altar. First go and be reconciled to them; then come and offer your gift."[1]

I've heard that rabbis in Jesus' day used to debate this question: If you have begun one duty, when is it right to interrupt it to do something else? The consensus was you could interrupt one duty only if there was a higher and more important duty you were neglecting. Since worshiping God is an incredibly high and important duty, I would expect Jesus to say you don't interrupt it for anything. But that's not what Jesus said. He said if you're *at church* and you realize that you have a fractured relationship, if there's someone with animosity toward you, leave church and deal with that person. Do whatever you can to make things right with that person, then come back and worship God.

So we could actually be at church, worshiping God, and, like Herb, be at the wrong place, doing the wrong thing.

This is why our fourth step is "With God's help, I always forgive and ask to be forgiven."

We've talked about offering forgiveness, but we need to ask for it as well. If we're going to move past our past and into the future God has for us, we need to do what we can to reconcile our relationships and make things right.

Making the Correction

Have you ever looked at the "corrections" section in the newspaper? This is where the paper admits errors they've made and seeks to make them right. Some are hysterical. Have fun reading these:

Walmart: Police receive a report of a newborn infant found in a trash can. Upon investigation, officers discover it was only a burrito.

Due to a typing error, Saturday's story on local artist Jon Henninger mistakenly reported that Henninger's band mate Eric Lyday was on drugs. The story should have read that Lyday was on drums. The Sentinel regrets the error.

A headline on an item in the Feb. 5 edition of the Enquirer-Bulletin incorrectly stated "Stolen groceries." It should have read "Homicide."

Wow.

In each of these situations, the newspaper made a mistake, realized it, and sought to correct it.

One time Jesus was traveling, and he "entered Jericho and was passing through."[2] He had no plans to stop and spend time in Jericho, which would have disappointed the people living there. At the time, Jesus was kind of a big deal. The people would have loved for him to stay and would have chosen a highly respected person to host him to bring honor to their town.

Since Jesus wasn't staying, the people lined the streets going into, going through, and coming out of Jericho. A man named Zacchaeus wanted to see Jesus, but the crowd was too thick and he was too short, so he climbed a sycamore tree to get a peek at Jesus when he passed by. The fact that it's a sycamore tree helps us know that Jesus had already gone through the town and was on his way out, because there was an ancient instruction in what was called the Mishnah that a sycamore tree had to be grown at least fifty cubits outside of a village.

There was a second reason Zacchaeus was in the tree. He was probably hiding. Zacchaeus was the chief tax collector in Jericho, which made him the most despised man in town. It's not just that he collected people's taxes; it's what he collected them for. At the time, Rome was seeking to take over the world, and even Israel was occupied by Roman forces and under their control. Once Rome asserted its authority, it taxed the people. Rome employed local Jews who would work for the

Romans collecting the taxes. Some historians estimate that the Jews at the time of Jesus may have been paying up to 80 or 90 percent of their income in taxes to Rome. Why? To fund Rome's massive army—the very army that was oppressing them! And Zacchaeus was one of the Jews aiding and abetting the Romans. He had betrayed God and betrayed God's people by taking a position as tax collector for Rome.

Not only that, tax collectors demanded more from the people than Rome required, keeping the extra for themselves. It was so bad that one village built a statue to an honest tax collector.

Tax collectors were deemed the lowest of the low. They were considered spiritually unclean because of their close interaction with the Romans and with Roman currency (which bore images of Caesar), so you couldn't touch them or enter their homes or eat with them, or you would become unclean too.

Zacchaeus wasn't just any tax collector. He was the *chief* tax collector. He was kind of like the head of the mafia, and he had become wealthy from taking advantage of other people. Those "other people" wished he would die.

Zacchaeus was in a tree hiding. He was in the wrong place, doing the wrong thing.

Jesus passed through Jericho, then stopped and looked up into the tree. Everyone followed his gaze, and that's when they spotted Zacchaeus, sitting on a branch like a monkey. Jesus opened his mouth to speak, and everyone knew exactly what he'd say. "Zacchaeus, you have betrayed God and these people. I condemn you for your sins." Or maybe, "Hello, Zacchaeus. My name is Jesus. You betrayed my Father. Prepare to die!'*"

But that's *not* what Jesus said. He said, "Zacchaeus! Quick, come down! I must be a guest in your home today." Zacchaeus climbed down and took Jesus to his home "in great excitement and joy."[3] No one in the crowd was feeling excitement and joy. They were *angry*. "'He has gone to be the guest of a notorious sinner,' they grumbled."[4]

---

* A little shout-out to fans of *The Princess Bride*.

Soon Jesus and Zacchaeus were having dinner, and I wonder if the crowd followed and watched. It wouldn't have been unusual. At the time, dinners at the homes of wealthy people were often observed by the public.

During the dinner, Zacchaeus realized that despite his sin, Jesus was showing him kindness and offering forgiveness. And around his house he saw the faces of people he had cheated and wronged, people who were hurting because of his lack of kindness. Then finally, there was a collision. God's heart of grace toward him smashed into his heart of greed and "Zacchaeus stood before the Lord and said, 'I will give half my wealth to the poor, Lord, and if I have cheated people on their taxes, I will give them back four times as much!'"[5]

Zacchaeus realized he could not receive God's forgiveness while not asking for forgiveness from others. Jesus sought to reconcile Zacchaeus with God and that, by necessity, meant he had to be reconciled to others. He knew he had made mistakes, and it was time to correct them.

Can you imagine if he didn't? What if Zacchaeus had accepted God's forgiveness and gotten right with God but never sought the forgiveness of and gotten right with others? He would have led a completely incongruent life, and his ability to grow in God's grace would have been severely stunted because he wouldn't have had a community of people to support and encourage him.

Zacchaeus made amends, and we need to as well. We need to

- make a list of the people we have wronged;
- own up to the wrong; and
- do what we can to make the wrong right.

Before you go to the person you've harmed (yes, I'm talking about actually going to the person you've harmed), ask God to change your heart. You need to go in true repentance and humility, or your apology may do more harm than good.

You may want to do a role reversal. Think about how you would want someone who has wronged you to make amends with you. I bet you wouldn't want to hear justifications or promises about the future. You'd probably hope they'd come in a spirit of brokenness, with a simple "I was wrong. I am so sorry. Is there any way I can make this right?"

It requires courage to take this step. It may feel like more courage than you have, but you need to do it. The only reason not to do it is if, after praying and seeking advice from someone you trust, you honestly believe that going to the person would do more harm than good. But this should be an exception, not the rule.

I realize this sounds intimidating, but you will be so glad you did it, because it will change your life.

There will be benefits to your *emotional health*. One reason people can't forgive themselves is that they carry the burden of pain they've caused other people. Admitting our wrong and asking for forgiveness helps to remove the burden.

Making amends also has obvious benefits for your *relational health*. As a pastor I repeatedly have conversations with husbands who are carrying grudges against their wives, people who are bitter toward their parents, siblings who haven't even spoken to each other in years because of some fight. I know Rodney King would ask, "Can we all just get along?" But the real question is, "Can someone just apologize?" Will someone be man or woman enough to let go of pride, admit wrongdoing, and try to make amends?

Making amends will also benefit your *spiritual health*. It's really difficult to be spiritually healthy when you're not relationally healthy.

When our relationships with people are dysfunctional, our relationship with God gets disrupted. It's not that God loves us less, but there will be interference in our relationship with him. It only makes sense. I've got two kids. If they're screaming at each other, or bitter and not talking, nothing in our home is going to be the same. I'll still love my kids just as much, but my relationship with each will be stressed because their relationship with each other is stressed.

It may sound intimidating, and it may take great courage, but you need to ask for forgiveness from the people you've hurt. You'll be glad you did.

If you're reading this book and you have relationships where there's animosity, where you've wronged someone and not made things right, then you are in the wrong place, doing the wrong thing.

You need to take off your noise-canceling headphones and listen for God's voice. If you do, you'll hear him saying, "Herb?" (I guess only if your name is Herb.) "Herb! You are not where you are supposed to be. I need you to make your wrongs right. You need to do that. Herb, where are you?"

It's time to wake up and do the right thing.

* * *

I know it's not easy to approach that person. Maybe you've already decided you aren't going to do that. Can I just say . . . you aren't going to actually find restoration without doing it. Maybe you need some other people to encourage you. Maybe you need to hear some success stories to motivate you. You can find those at TheRestoreCommunity.com. It's a free community of people who are all looking to break out of their pasts and into God's future.

THE TOP TEN SIGNS YOUR INNER CHILD IS UPSET

10. He's been bullying all your friends' inner children.

9. He dropped out of inner high school to create a heart palpitation.

8. He's an inner lawyer and slaps you with a $40 million inner lawsuit.

7. You're thinking about getting him an inner puppy to make him happy.

6. He hasn't touched his inner train set for days.

5. He's wearing all black and has a new emo haircut.

4. He's throwing a tantrum because his inner little sister pushed the buttons in the elevator, and it was *his* turn!

3. He refuses to pick up his inner laundry off his inner bedroom floor and put it in the inner hamper.

2. He's joined an inner gang and goes wilding through your pancreas.

1. He's holding his breath until he gets his way.

I STAY CONNECTED TO GOD AND OTHERS

Remember that whole

"I can't" deal?

Turns out

it's more than a decision.

It has to become

a way of life.

If I truly believe "I can't,"

I wouldn't think of

trying to live my life alone.

That's why I need to

stay connected

to God

and others.

LIVING OUT OF YOUR LIMBIC

ABOUT A MONTH INTO my junior year of high school I marched into my guidance counselor's office and announced, "I am quitting chemistry."

"Now wait a second," he said, trying to slow me down. "Why would you do that?"

"Because I hate learning about science."

"What?" My guidance counselor seemed confused. "Why do you hate learning about science?"

"Because I'm not a nerd."

"Now hold on." He seemed to be moving from confused to concerned. "What if someday you need to know chemistry for your job?"

"I won't. I'm going to be a lawyer."

"Well, but then—" my guidance counselor seemed to think he had a winning argument—"what if you need to know chemistry for one of your law cases?"

"Then I'll hire a nerd chemist."

Game. Set. Match.

I quit chemistry.

I hate learning about science.

Will You or Won't You?

You've made a decision. You are no longer going to do . . . whatever it is you've been doing. You're going to find freedom and overcome your addictive behavior, your hurt, your bad habit.

But will you? Will you really?

To overcome your addiction you need to rely on God. You're not going to overcome your addiction; *God is*. We've already established that you can't but God can. That is not just a realization you have or a decision you make; it has to be a moment-by-moment reality you choose to live in. So when temptation hits, your response is *not* to call upon all the willpower you can muster; it's to call upon God. Your response is, "God, I know I can't do this. I've proved a thousand times that I don't have the power to do what I want to do. But *you* have the power. I know you love me. I know you want freedom for me, and you have a better life for me. I need your power right now. I am saying no to this in your power, God."

To overcome your addiction, you need to rely on God.

More specifically, you need to rely on God in a way that works. You need to work with the way your brain works. Let's be honest. Lots of people want to overcome their addictions, hurts, and bad habits but *don't*. Lots of people decide they're going to rely on God when the moment of temptation strikes but *don't*.

So why will you succeed?

Because you're going to rely on God in a way that corresponds with the way you were designed. If you don't work with the way your brain works, you will constantly be in a war against yourself, and that's not a battle you're likely to win. In fact, that's exactly what many of us have been doing, and we've been losing.

That's right: to find and live in freedom, as much as I hate to admit it, we need to learn some science.

This Is Your Brain

I'm going to explain the way your brain works in a somewhat basic way, partly because I don't want to bore you with a very technical explanation and lots of hard-to-pronounce words, and partly because I dropped out of chemistry, so my ability to grasp and communicate all of this is limited.*

Trust me: this is fascinating and *critical* for you to understand.

Your brain is divided into sections. Each section has its own responsibility. That's why someone who has a brain injury may no longer be able to tie his shoes, or talk, or recognize his own family, or use his legs. It depends on which part of the brain was injured and what function that part plays.

The limbic brain is responsible for our awareness of external stimuli and our responses to them. The limbic brain is also the part of the brain that generates our feelings, like trust, love, loyalty, and compassion. The limbic brain is involved in decision making as well.

Interestingly, this part of your brain has no capacity for logic. Yes, that's right, the part of your brain that has so much influence on the decisions you make cannot think logically. That's why you may make a decision that just "feels right."

Your limbic brain also has no capacity for language. That's why you may feel certain things but have trouble describing them. A friend asks, "Why do you love him?" You answer, "I don't know; I just do." She asks again, "But why?" You struggle. "Well . . . he's funny and . . . he's smart." She presses, "Okay, but there are lots of men who are funny and smart. Do you love them?" You get frustrated. "No, I love just *him*."

It's hard to explain your feelings because the part of your brain

---

* My guidance counselor was right—I *do* need science for my job!

that feels emotion isn't capable of language. This is why when you try to describe feelings, you can say things that really don't make a lot of sense. "He, well, he, completes me." Your friend laughs. "*That's* why you love him, because he completes you? Could you explain what that means?" You quit trying. "No, I can't."

There's another section of your brain called the neocortex. It's around the outside of your brain. It's the part of your brain that's responsible for rational and analytical thought, where you weigh pros and cons and reason things out. The neocortex is also responsible for language. It has no capacity for feelings. The neocortex can inform your decisions by applying logic, but it does not *make* your decisions. The emotional, feeling, limbic brain makes your decisions.

When presented with a choice, what often happens is that you have an instantaneous (limbic) reaction. Then your neocortex comes into play, seeking to apply logic to your assessment. Your neocortex may talk you out of your first instinct or convince you that you were right, but ultimately your limbic brain will make the choice.

This Is Your Brain in Recovery

If you've made the decision to move past your past and get free of your junk *and* if you've made the decision that you can't but God can (so you've given your life to his will), then your first instinct should probably be right, right? That limbic, emotional, initial response should coincide with the heart decision you've made. We could say your first instinct should now likely be your God instinct.

The Bible describes the transformation that happens in our minds when we surrender our lives to God and his will:

> Those who live according to the flesh have their minds set on what the flesh desires; but those who live in accordance with the Spirit have their minds set on what the Spirit desires.[1]

And:

> Therefore, I urge you, brothers and sisters, in view of God's
> mercy, to offer your bodies as a living sacrifice, holy and
> pleasing to God—this is your true and proper worship. Do
> not conform any longer to the pattern of this world, but be
> transformed by the renewing of your mind. Then you will
> be able to test and approve what God's will is—his good,
> pleasing and perfect will.[2]

What we want and need is a (limbic) brain that's been "renewed"
and is set on what God desires for our lives. What we want is a limbic
brain that is working *with* us, not *against* us. And the way we do that
is through prayer.

This Is Your Brain on Prayer

Let's get clear on what prayer is.

Prayer is more than just presenting a list of requests to God. God
loves us and cares about every detail of our lives, so he *does* invite us
to present requests to him. But prayer is a lot more than that.

Prayer is living in the presence of and accessing the power of God.
Prayer is me deciding to think God thoughts instead of me thoughts.
Prayer is breathing in God's love and resting in God's strength.

If prayer is just telling God what we need, there are a bunch of
verses in the Bible that make no sense to me. Verses like:

- "Never stop praying."[3]
- "I know the LORD is always with me. I will not be shaken, for
  he is right beside me."[4]
- "Pray in the Spirit at all times and on every occasion."[5]
- "As for me, how good it is to be near God! I have made the
  Sovereign LORD my shelter."[6]
- "You will show me the way of life, granting me the joy of your
  presence and the pleasures of living with you forever."[7]

Prayer isn't just something we do to connect with God for a few minutes in the day; it's how we stay connected with God *every* minute of the day.

Prayer isn't something God commands us to do; it's something we *need* to do. We need to because "I can't; God can."

We need to pray because it's how we stay connected with God, receiving clarity on his will and his power to live it out.

We need to pray because it renews our mind, and it can change how our limbic brain perceives and responds to external stimuli, what feelings it generates, and ultimately what decisions it makes. When we pray, we're relying on God in a way that works because it works with the way our brains work.

This has been proved scientifically.*

For instance, in an article in the *Journal of Experimental Social Psychology*, professors Malt Friese and Michaela Wanke share studies that suggest that prayer increases a person's ability to resist temptation.[8] They aren't the first. Another study, led by Kevin Rounding from the psychology department at Queen's University in Canada, likewise showed that prayer replenishes willpower and bolsters self-control.[9] There's a problem, though—these professors are atheists. Not believing in God but then discovering that praying to God helps people puts you in a bind. It forces you to somehow explain the result away. Want to know how Friese and Wanke do it? They cite research demonstrating that social interactions give people the "cognitive resources necessary to avoid temptation."† They then come to the conclusion that people who pray interpret it as social interaction with God, and *that's* what gives them power over their temptations. They postulate that any social interaction, including silent social interaction with an imaginary deity, will help a person's self-control.

Okay.

---

* Stupid science!
† That's true, and we'll be talking about it in a couple of chapters.

Or maybe God is real, really loves us, and really helps us when we call on him.

There are other scientific findings that may help us to understand how prayer helps us and how relying on God through prayer works with the way our limbic brain works. Yale professor John Bargh conducted experiments on unsuspecting undergraduates to better understand how our brains function.[10] He especially studied what he calls "priming." If you've ever put a coat of primer on a wall before painting it, you know you can't see the primer, but it's right there underneath what you can see. What you *can* see is different because of what you *can't* see. Bargh suggested that, in a similar way, we can prime our minds.

One of his experiments involved a scrambled-sentence test. One group of students took a test sprinkled with rude words like *disturb*, *bother*, and *intrude*. Another group took a test sprinkled with polite words like *respect*, *considerate*, and *yield*. The groups had no idea about the covert word placement; they thought they were just taking an intelligence test. After taking the five-minute test, the students were asked, individually, to walk down the hall and talk to the professor about their next assignment. The professor was intentionally engaged in conversation with someone when the students arrived. The question was how long it would take the students to interrupt. It turned out that the students primed with rude words interrupted, on average, after five minutes. But 82 percent of those primed with polite words *never* interrupted at all. The students didn't pick up on the word trend in the test consciously, but their brains were primed by it subconsciously, and it affected their decision making and their behavior afterward.

Two Dutch researchers conducted a similar experiment by asking a group of students forty-two Trivial Pursuit questions.[11] Before receiving the questions, half of the subjects were asked to take five minutes to think about what life would be like if they were university professors. The other half were asked to spend five minutes thinking about soccer.

The soccer group got 42.6 percent of the Trivial Pursuit questions correct.

The professor group got 55.6 percent of the Trivial Pursuit questions correct.

The professor group wasn't smarter; they were just primed with smart thoughts.

So why does prayer help people overcome temptation? One reason is because it works with the way our brains work. When we pray, we are thinking God thoughts. Those God thoughts prime our brains. Then, when we encounter an external stimulus that in the past would have triggered an instantaneous (limbic) selfish or sinful or self-defeating thought, instead it is *far* more likely that it will trigger a God thought. Why? Because, by praying, we've primed our brains with God thoughts.

So . . . pray.

If you want to be free, if you want to stop doing the thing you haven't been able to stop doing, or want to start doing the thing you haven't been doing, *pray*.

When you wake up, pray. Start priming your mind with God thoughts immediately.

Then, throughout your day, keep praying. I struggle to bring my thoughts back to God. (I blame my ADD.*) One thing that has helped me is setting the alarm on my phone to go off almost every hour. I'm reminded to pray each day at 8:08, 9:09, 10:10, 11:11, 12:12, 1:11, 2:22, 3:33, 4:44, 7:07, 8:08, and 9:09.

I love the advice Max Lucado gives in his book *Just like Jesus*. He suggests that you first give God your *waking* thoughts. When you wake in the morning, focus your initial thoughts on him. Then give God your *waiting* thoughts. Spend some quiet time with God, sharing your heart with him and listening for his voice. Third, give God your *whispering* thoughts. The idea is to repeatedly offer up brief prayers throughout the day. You might repeat the same short

---

* Which, come to think of it, may be another reason I quit chemistry.

prayer—"God, I need you" or "Am I in your will, Lord?" or "I can't, God, but you can." Then, last, give God your *waning* thoughts. Talk to God as you're falling asleep.[12]

If you're going to live out your decision to find freedom and overcome your addictive behavior, your hurt, and your bad habit, then you're going to have to stay connected to God.

You have to pray.

And when you pray, you're priming your limbic brain.

CREATING NEW RUTS

LIVING IN THE OLD WEST, my family rides horses pretty much everywhere we go.

Okay, not *everywhere* we go.

Okay, we went horseback riding *one time*, but the horses taught me an important lesson.

We were riding in a line—an old cowboy instructor guy, then the four of us from my family, then another old cowboy instructor guy. There was a narrow rut that made a path through the desert. I'm guessing the rut was maybe six to eight inches wide and about four inches deep. With every step each of the six horses took, they placed each hoof in the rut. I watched and realized their hooves *never* landed outside the rut. It looked awkward and difficult, so I finally asked old cowboy instructor guy #2, "Why do you make your horses walk in this rut?"

"Oh, we don't make 'em, Partner,'"* he explained. "They made the rut themselves. Ever since the first time we took 'em out, they put their hooves in exactly the same place, every time. Over time that made the rut, and they're still putting their hooves in the same place they always have."

I imagined twenty years into the future, the rut now forty feet deep, the horses having to wear coal miner helmets so they could see their way through the dark, cavernous gorge they had doomed themselves to.

I couldn't decide whether I found the whole thing funny or sad. Then I realized, *I am just like those horses.* Their problem is my problem. Then it was time to stop and eat lunch, so I stopped thinking about it altogether because, yum, lunch!

Triggers

We'll think about those horses and their rut more in a minute, but first it's time to learn about triggers.

If you spent time at rehab, counselors would teach you that identifying and overcoming triggers is paramount in your recovery. A trigger is a stimulus that gives you the desire or justification to return to the addictive behavior you want to put behind you. Triggers may include your mind-set about your recovery—for instance, feeling overconfident or full of self-pity or like the journey to recovery is taking too long. Triggers may be emotional, such as stress, depression, loneliness, anxiety, or fear. Triggers are often more circumstantial, like hanging out with a certain group of friends or at a specific place or being hungry or tired.

Your rehab counselor would teach you to identify your triggers and then, when you leave the treatment center, to avoid your triggers whenever possible. So, if you're an alcoholic, stay out of bars and away from your friends who want to party with them. If you're a

---

* I don't remember if he really called me "Partner," but I thought that gave a nice cowboy feel to the dialogue. Hope you enjoy!

gambling addict, stay out of casinos. If you're a crack addict, going in a crack house isn't the best strategy to maintain your sobriety.

Part of our recovery journey needs to be identifying and then avoiding our triggers. I would strongly encourage you to do that. In fact, you may want to put this book down and take some time to identify your triggers now.

But at the same time, because this is rehab *for the rest of us*, it may be a bit more complicated for you. The problem is that your issue may be more socially acceptable and therefore easy to identify but difficult or even impossible to avoid. For instance:

- If your struggle is with gossip, and your trigger is talking to other people, well, you can't just stay away from other people.
- If your struggle is with forgiving your spouse, and your trigger is your spouse, you can't stay away from him or her.
- If your struggle is with lust, you can get software on your computer, but there are always going to be people you can look at lustfully. You can't stay away from them.
- If your struggle is self-loathing and negative self-talk, you can't stay away from yourself!

So if you can avoid your triggers, great. But if you can't, you need another strategy. Good news: there is one. To implement it in our lives, we need to understand . . . our brains. Yep, it's time for another science lesson!

The Con

First, let's review.

Remember, your brain is divided into sections, each with its own responsibility.

An inner section called your limbic brain is responsible for your awareness of and reactions to external stimuli. It's the section that generates feelings but has no capacity for logic or language.

An outer part of your brain called the neocortex is responsible for logic and analytical thought and language. The neocortex seeks to inform your decisions, but the limbic brain is still going to call the shots.

We said that once you've made the decision to not engage in your self-destructive thinking or behavior anymore, when you encounter a trigger, your first (limbic) feeling and response should be "No," especially when you prime your brain with prayer. Your initial instinct can become, "I made a decision about that. I don't want to be that person anymore." If, recognizing you are God's child, you sincerely gave your life to his will, I think we could even say your first instinct can become more than just a good instinct; it can be your God instinct.

All good so far, but remember, your neocortex is going to speak into your final decision. This is where the problem comes in. Because when it comes to your addictive behavior or thinking, your neocortex is not always going to be your friend. Your neocortex will often be like a street hustler. Picture a shady, persuasive, smooth-talking con artist trying to get a teenager from the neighborhood to try a gateway drug or to get in the back of his van. Your neocortex will try to hustle you and convince you that engaging in what you swore you'd never do again is completely justifiable. In fact, he'll tell you it's expected, and it would be weird—you would almost be *wrong*—not to do it.

I told you a few chapters back that in the course of studying for and writing this book, I recognized that I have an issue with food. I eat unhealthy types and amounts of food. Hunger has nothing to do with my eating; I eat to eat. When I recognized my problem and that "I can't; God can," I made a decision: "I'm not going to eat unhealthy foods. I'm not going to overeat. I'm not going to eat when I'm not hungry."

One of my main triggers is . . . *food*. Unfortunately, I can't avoid food.* I still see food. But I've made a decision, and I've noticed that

---

* Well, I guess I could. But death would occur somewhere around week seven or eight of my avoiding food.

my first instinct has changed. Whereas I used to think, *Food! Yeah! Let's do this!* my response now is *No. I made a decision that I'm going to eat healthy foods, and only when I'm hungry.*

Cool, right?

Yeah, it is.

But then my neocortex starts his hustle, and things can get ugly fast. Here's how it can go for me. We have family come into town. I realize there will be the opportunity for me to eat poorly when we go out to a restaurant. My first instinct is, *No. I'm not going to eat unhealthily.* Then my neocortex comes slithering up all sly, *But this is an exception. You can stick to your decision but have some exceptions, and this is definitely one of them. You're not going to deprive your guests because of your problem, are you? C'mon, you can do it, just this once,* and I find myself carrying my third plate of food back to the table at the all-you-can-eat buffet.[*]

I have to travel out of town. I realize it will be easy for me to eat poorly on the road. My first instinct is *No, I'm not going to eat unhealthily.* Then my neocortex whispers, *But this is an exception. How can you eat healthily when you're having lunch in an airport and dinner in a hotel? You'll get back to eating healthily when you get home. For now, I think I saw a pizza place in the airport food court. It's okay. Really. You can do it just this once.* I find myself ordering two pieces of meat lover's pizza. *You know what, if I'm going to eat pizza, why even pretend I'm eating healthily? So I think I will add some garlic knots.*

There is a cake at a special event at our church. My first instinct is *No, I'm not going to eat unhealthily.* Then my neocortex gets all seductive. *But this is an exception. It's a celebration! You're not going to sit it out. Don't you have a right to celebrate? You deserve this. Besides, everyone else is. You don't want to be the one weird cakeless guy. What would people think? That you're not into the celebration—that's what they would think.*

---

[*] I live in Las Vegas. Baltimore is famous for crabs. If you go to Texas, you eat barbecue. Louisville is known for the hot brown sandwich. Las Vegas's contribution to the culinary world is perfecting the all-you-can-eat buffet.

So grab a piece of cake. You can do it just this once. I find myself eating a piece of cake. Or two.

The next day I see that there is leftover cake in the office. My first instinct is, *No, I'm not going to eat unhealthily.* Then my neocortex starts his hustle. *But this is an exception. How many times is there leftover cake in the office? This is the only time! So eating that cake isn't going to become a habit. Besides, you don't want the cake to go to waste. You can do it just this once,* and I find myself eating another piece of cake.

By my count, "just this once" happens four or five times a week.

Ruts

I'm guessing you can identify with my struggle. It may not be food for you, but you understand making a decision, then encountering a trigger, having the initial desire to do the right thing, but finding yourself rationalizing why you can do what you swore you would no longer do.

I'm making the process sound kind of funny, like there's a cartoon drug pusher prowling around your brain, but it's not funny. It's real. You can understand the reality of it regardless of whether you're someone who takes more of a spiritual or more of a scientific approach to life.*

Spiritually, the Bible warns us that when we want to do right, we will experience a force pressing us to do wrong, specifically through deceiving our minds:

> I have discovered this principle of life—that when I want to do what is right, I inevitably do what is wrong. I love God's law with all my heart. But there is another power within me that is at war with my mind. This power makes me a slave to the sin that is still within me.[1]

---

* Do not read that sentence as me implying that science and spirituality are at odds with each other. They are not.

Stay alert! Watch out for your great enemy, the devil. He prowls around like a roaring lion, looking for someone to devour.[2]

I fear that somehow your pure and undivided devotion to Christ will be corrupted, just as Eve was deceived by the cunning ways of the serpent.[3]

Scientifically, we would understand the conniving power of the neocortex as the presence of neural pathways in our brains. If we're going to move past our self-destructive behaviors and thinking, we *have to* understand neural pathways and have a strategy to overcome them. I'll try to explain neural pathways, but remember, I dropped out of science, so this is going to be pretty basic.

The way your brain thinks and directs the parts of your body is through neurons. Neurons "link" together to create messages. The first time a particular type of message is sent, it will result in an awkward experience for you. Picture walking through a forest you've never been in. You would be unsure of yourself and where to put your feet. A similar thing happens in your brain when you try something for the first time. Now picture walking through the same part of the same forest again, and then again, and again. Each time it would become easier. In fact, you would quickly start to form a path through that forest. That's a great analogy for what happens with your brain. The more you do something, the more natural it becomes because you are literally forming a neural pathway in your brain. You're developing a rut that will become very easy to fall into. In fact, it will eventually become very difficult *not* to fall into that rut.

Neural pathways are often a good thing. Picture learning how to play the piano. At first you carefully place your fingers in the right places, and reading the music and having your fingers go to the right keys is clumsy at best, seemingly impossible at worst. But as you practice and take lessons, your skill level grows, and you're able to play naturally and gracefully. Why? Did your fingers become better fingers? No. What happened was you developed neural pathways. Eventually you'd be able to play the piano without even thinking about it. You could even talk to someone about Kanye West's latest tweet rampage as you played the piano. Why? Because playing the piano has become a rut you fall into. You developed the right neural pathways, and so while it used to be almost impossible to play the piano skillfully, now it's almost impossible for you not to.

Neural pathways can also be a bad thing. Neural pathways are how addictions develop. The first time you respond to stress by drinking a glass of wine or try to impress other people by exaggerating about yourself or click on a link that takes you to pictures of scantily clad women, it feels awkward. Maybe you feel guilty at first. But the experience gives you a little jolt of pleasure. So even though you may not feel right about what you've done, it did feel kind of good. You try it again. This time doing so is a bit less clumsy. The third time it's even easier. Why? You're developing a neural pathway. Do the same thing enough times, and you will have a rut that it's almost impossible for you not to fall into. *That's* your addiction.

New Ruts

What do we do about our swindling con-artist neocortex? How do we overcome the spiritual force opposed to us becoming free? Is there a way to break out of the neural pathway our brain has locked, loaded, and ready for us any time we come across one of our triggers?

Yep. We need new ruts.

It won't work to just say, "I'm not going to keep living according to my same self-defeating patterns!" Sorry, honey, you're always going to live according to patterns.

It won't work to say, "I'm not going to keep falling into my same old stupid habits!" Sorry, bro, you were designed to fall into habits.

Just choosing to muster up your willpower or even trying to rely on God's power is not enough because you will be working against the way your brain works. Again, you need a plan that works according to the way your brain works. You need new ruts.

How do you create them?

The best way I know (actually the *only* way I know) is through memorizing "signature" Bible verses that apply to your signature sin.

The problem is that your neocortex* will seek to justify you going back to old behavior by convincing you of lies. The way you combat lies is with truth. God's Word is truth,[4] and it can help us confront the deception and establish new neural pathways that we automatically fall into.

The Bible tells us we need to "demolish arguments and every pretension that sets itself up against the knowledge of God, and we take captive every thought to make it obedient to Christ."[5] How do we do that? We confront and overcome lies with truth. That's what we see Jesus do when he was tempted. Each time he was confronted with a lie that pushed him toward sin, he responded by quoting a Bible verse he had memorized.[6] That's what we are told to do as well: "I have hidden your word in my heart, that I might not sin against you."[7]

We need to not just know but *memorize* Bible verses. I'm going to suggest memorizing a sequence of strategic Bible verses in a specific order—because we are seeking to create a new neural pathway so our neocortex response is to apply God's truth to the situation, rather than the old lies we've always lived by. We're converting our neocortex from hustler to preacher.

Remember, we made the decision "I can't; God can." So now we're seeking to make that our moment-by-moment reality through staying connected to God. We stay connected to God through prayer but also through remembering his words. So we're going to use Bible verses to create new ruts that we automatically fall into when we come across one of our triggers.

For instance, I recognized I have an issue with food. So what did I do?

---

* Assisted by Satan or your established neural pathways.

I had the realization. *I've got a problem. I don't want to continue living like this.* I made a decision. *I can't, but God can, so I give this area of my life to his will.*

But that will not work on its own.

I need to stay connected to God and make it a reality I live in, not just a realization I've had or a decision I've made.

So I started praying, priming my mind and conditioning my limbic brain.

And I found Bible verses that apply to my issue:

Don't you realize that your body is the temple of the Holy Spirit, who lives in you and was given to you by God? You do not belong to yourself, for God bought you with a high price. So you must honor God with your body.[8]

You say, "I am allowed to do anything"—but not everything is good for you. And even though "I am allowed to do anything," I must not become a slave to anything.[9]

That is why I tell you not to worry about everyday life—whether you have enough food and drink, or enough clothes to wear. Isn't life more than food, and your body more than clothing?[10]

Jesus replied, "I am the bread of life. Whoever comes to me will never be hungry again. Whoever believes in me will never be thirsty."[11]

Jesus explained: "My nourishment comes from doing the will of God, who sent me, and from finishing his work."[12]

They are headed for destruction. Their god is their appetite, they brag about shameful things, and they think only about this life here on earth. But we are citizens of heaven, where the Lord Jesus Christ lives. And we are eagerly waiting for him to return as our Savior.[13]

I am currently working on memorizing those verses so that remembering them isn't awkward but automatic. When visitors come into town, or I'm out of town, or some devil woman at church brings in a chocolate cake, instead of thinking of deceptive rationalizations for why I can, I want to automatically fall into thinking truthful God thoughts that will empower me to do what I really want to do. *

Your problem may not be food, so what might this look like for you?

Let's say you have an issue with buying things you don't need and can't afford. You're walking through the mall and see this great new thing you'd love to have. Your old rut would have been to justify how other people have nice things, and you shouldn't be the only one deprived, and spending a few hundred bucks on that isn't going to sink you into bankruptcy, and you find yourself standing in line holding your credit card. But now you've created a new rut to fall into. So when you see that great new thing to buy, you find yourself thinking, "True godliness with contentment is itself great wealth. After all, we brought nothing with us when we came into the world, and we can't take anything with us when we leave it. So if we have enough food and clothing, let us be content."[14] And then, "Wherever your treasure is, there the desires of your heart will also be."[15] And then, "Don't store up treasures here on earth, where moths eat them and rust destroys them, and where thieves break in and steal. Store your treasures in heaven, where moths and rust cannot destroy, and thieves do not break in and steal."[16] You find that you have walked past the store, and you thank God for his help with the final verse of your signature sequence: "For I can do everything through Christ, who gives me strength."[17]

---

* And just FYI: I went out of town recently and asked the guy who picked me up at the airport to let me run into a grocery store, where I bought blueberries, Greek yogurt, and sliced chicken breast. And this week when we had sheet cakes celebrating our church's birthday, and the next day when there was leftover cake in the office, I did *not* eat a piece. Take that, neocortex! Bam!

Or let's say your issue is with lust, and you're hit by one of your triggers. You know exactly what you would have thought before, but you now have a new rut to fall into. You tell yourself, *I can't even look because* "anyone who even looks at a woman with lust has already committed adultery with her in his heart"[18] *and* "I made a covenant with my eyes not to look with lust at a young woman."[19]

See what happened?

You *are* going to come across triggers, and you *will* fall into a pattern, but you've created a new rut to fall into. That's powerful! It works. You can do it. It's one of the ways you stay connected to God.

To overcome, you have to stay connected to God.

But God isn't the only one you have to stay connected to. . . .

RATS IN A CAGE

IT'S TRUE, but you're not going to believe me. Ready? Some sicko got a bunch of rats addicted to heroin.

You probably have a lot of questions. Did he get them hooked on a gateway drug to start? Maybe he first sold them marijuana and taught the rats how to roll their own joints? Did the guy throw big parties for rats and offer them heroin in the bathrooms? Were there any vice cop rats, working undercover as druggies, just waiting for the big transaction to bring the whole operation down?

I don't know all of the answers to those outstanding questions.

Here's what I do know. For years experiments were done where scientists put a lone rat in a cage and gave it two water bottles. One was filled with water. The other contained water laced with morphine.* The rat chose morphine and quickly became addicted. In no

---

* Heroin is basically liquefied morphine.

time it was pawning off all its possessions for drug money and waking up with a face tattoo.

The scientist conducting the experiment (i.e., the dealer) said the rat proved that drugs cause addiction. Drugs, it was said, have "hooks" that are inescapable.

In the late 1970s a professor named Bruce Alexander questioned that commonly held belief. And it *is* questionable. For instance, when people go into a hospital for surgery, they are often put on diacetyl-morphine. Diacetylmorphine is heroin. But patients don't come out addicted to it. You've probably had a grandparent who fell down the stairs, had surgery, was put on diacetylmorphine—maybe even for twenty straight days—but came off it with no addiction. Why isn't your grandma a heroin junkie?

Alexander's hypothesis was that the reason the rats chose the drug water was because "severely distressed animals, like severely distressed people, will relieve their distress pharmacologically if they can."[1]

To test his hypothesis, Alexander built "Rat Park." Rat Park was like Disneyland for rats.* It contained sixteen to twenty rats, food, balls, wheels, and tubes. As in the previous experiments, two water bottles were offered. One water bottle had water; the other water was laced with morphine. But unlike in the lone-rat-in-a-cage experiments, almost no rats chose the drug water, virtually no rats became addicted, and none overdosed. In the previous experiment, almost *every* rat overdosed.

So what's going on?

A professor from the Netherlands named Peter Cohen, commenting on these results, said, "We should stop talking about 'addiction' altogether, and instead call it 'bonding.'"[2] The idea is that humans have a natural need to bond. We are supposed to bond with each other. But Cohen postulates that if something gets in the way of that, we'll bond with something else that will provide some sense of relief.

---

* Considering the fact that Mickey Mouse is, in fact, a rat, he would probably prefer Rat Park to Disneyland. Just sayin'.

For you it might be a video game or a Netflix series or beer or your phone or prescription drugs or gambling.

Because of the abuse I suffered from my father, bonding with other people has always been the one thing I didn't want to do. I decided early on that if I let people in, they would hurt me. So I put up walls. But I have to bond. I have to connect to something; it's my nature. I now realize that's part of what's going on with me and food. If I'm not connecting with other people, I connect with ice cream.

So you don't want to live a life where you're dependent on some substance or activity? You don't want to struggle with addiction? Make friends.

Turns out people aren't healthy in isolation.

What If I'm Already Addicted?

Let's go back to Rat Park for a minute. This super-fly, drug-dealing, rat-poisoning pusher Professor Alexander also tried another version of his experiment. This time he put lone rats in solitary cages and forced them to consume morphine hydrochloride for fifty-seven consecutive days. They became raging addicts. They were then removed from their isolated existence and brought to Rat Park, where they immediately became part of a thriving rat community. As with their previous cage, Rat Park had two water bottles, so there was the choice of water or morphine water. Almost every drug-addicted rat chose the *plain* water. Some exhibited signs of withdrawal,* but even still, when surrounded by rat friends, they chose plain water.

Left alone for much longer, they would have overdosed and died. In Rat Park, they broke free of their addiction and regained a good life.

It's not just rats. For instance, 20 percent of the American soldiers who went to war in Vietnam used and became addicted to heroin. In a study done of those who got clean before returning to the United States, only 5 percent relapsed after returning home. Ninety-five

---

* I don't know what it says about me, but I would love to see a rat experiencing drug withdrawal. Little rat, shaking and sweating, cursing at the nurses: "I need my fix!"

percent stopped taking drugs completely when they returned to friends and family who loved them and provided the opportunity to return to a normal life.[3]

Turns out people don't heal in isolation.

Alicia is one of my favorite people, partly because she's really funny, and partly because she thinks she's even funnier than she is. Alicia didn't grow up in the greatest neighborhood, and she likes to play up the fact that she was raised in the ghetto, so she doesn't have to use proper grammar or good manners.

One of the other things I like about Alicia is that she's transparent. She tells it like it is. A couple of months ago I texted her, "What are you doing for Christmas?" Her response? "Crying."

She's actually coming over for dinner tonight with my family. I texted her and asked her to give me several options of meals she likes so I could choose one to make. Her response? "Steak and asparagus."

I'm not sure about the ghetto part, but Alicia really did have a rough childhood. When she was three years old, her grandfather began abusing her sexually. When you're that age and the abuser is your grandfather, you don't know what to do and don't feel like you can say anything. It went on for more than a decade.

That will really mess a person up, and it messed up Alicia. Specifically, it messed up her thinking about sex. It would for anyone. Exposed to abusive sex at such a vulnerable age, Alicia was confused, and one day when the world of pornography was presented to her, she stepped into it. What started as curiosity, partly driven by questions her grandfather's abuse couldn't help but raise, soon became more. In fact, Alicia realized one day that she was no longer looking at pornography; she was *addicted* to pornography. She almost couldn't *not* look at it. When she was stressed or lonely or anxious, it's what she turned to. What her grandfather had done left her wounded and wary of getting too close to other people, so she bonded with the images on her screen.

Another thing I love about Alicia is that she's not the type of person who is going to settle for a less-than life. She knew she had a problem, but she wasn't willing to continue living with her problem.

So Alicia decided she had to tell someone. I can't imagine the courage that must have taken. She told a friend or two, and she told me. With the support of friends who now knew her secret, she sought help. She went to a support group. She started seeing a counselor. She joined an online support group too.

For the first time in her life, Alicia is experiencing victory in an area of her life where all she had known was defeat. She's experiencing freedom in an area of her life where all she had known was bondage.

I asked Alicia the other day what the difference was. Why was she finally moving past her addiction? She said it was connecting to others. Each time she told her story, it was like her sin lost power over her. It was embarrassing to say the words out loud but essential in her healing. Looking back, she realizes that her secret had isolated her. As she tiptoed out of the shadow of her shame, she moved into the light of loving community. For the first time she realized that what had happened to her had also happened to others. For the first time she got to know people who were struggling with the same things she struggled with.

Turns out the drug-dealing professor and his druggie rats were right: people aren't healthy in isolation, and people don't heal in isolation.

THE TOP TEN SIGNS YOU NEED MORE FRIENDS

10. You offered to pay your Uber driver twenty dollars to "hang out."

9. Your imaginary friend won't even spend time with you.

8. You get really excited when someone you're dating breaks up with you by saying, "I just want to be friends."

7. You have a T-shirt that says, "I'm not with stupid, or with anyone else for that matter."

6. The only conversation you had today was with Siri.

5. The only signature in your high school yearbook is your chemistry teacher.

4. Mark Zuckerberg personally called you to ask you to stop using Facebook.

3. You won two tickets to Disneyland . . . so you went twice.

2. You went to a James Taylor concert. He began singing, "You've got a friend," then spotted you in the audience and stopped.

1. Your only follower on Twitter is your grandma.

THE FDF

I WANT TO TALK TO you about getting naked.

Completely naked.

I also hope this book might get sold in Christian bookstores.

So . . . I might have a problem.

Maybe what I'll do is talk about naked animals. Actually, even that may be pushing things a bit. Maybe we'll talk about *clothed* animals.

But first, let's remember where we are.

Connected

To move past our self-defeating thoughts and self-destructive behaviors, we need to stay connected to God and others.

As we saw with my friend Alicia (and lots of rats), addictions lose their power when we live in healthy community. In community I find healing; in isolation I never will.

Why is that true? Because in community I come to two critical epiphanies: I'm not alone, and I can't do it alone.

I'm Not Alone

A major problem with whatever you're hung up on is that you think no one else is hung up on it. It's easy to think, *I'm so alone. No one else would understand. People aren't in the same situation I'm in. If they were, they couldn't handle it either.*

If someone else had been abused like I was, they'd be doing this too.

If someone else were tempted like I am, they'd be doing this too.

If someone else had my friends, they'd be doing this too.

If someone else had been hurt like I was, they'd be doing this too.

Outside of you living in community and sharing your secret, do you know who is in a position to disagree with you or show you you're wrong? No one.

In community, as we share the truth about ourselves, we realize we're not alone. We are hit with the liberating truth God tells us in the Bible: "The temptations in your life are no different from what others experience. And God is faithful. He will not allow the temptation to be more than you can stand. When you are tempted, he will show you a way out so that you can endure."[1]

I realize that it's easier to keep relationships at a nice Teflon level and that it's scary to share your secrets. The good news is that *everyone* feels that way, and *everyone* has something they need to share. So if you, in a safe environment, open up, you'll find others opening up as well. As people start sharing, something magical will happen in that community. I love the way Heather Kopp, a recovering alcoholic and the author of *Sober Mercies*, says it: "People bond more deeply over shared brokenness than they do over shared beliefs."[2]

I Can't Do It Alone

As you open up and discover the liberating truth "I am not alone," you'll begin to experience the empowering truth "I can't do it alone."

Maybe for years you've struggled with feelings of bitterness or your addiction to prescription drugs or losing large sums of money on Internet poker or shame about your abortion, and you've tried to move past it but have not been able to. A big part of the reason is because you've been trying alone, and you can't do it alone.

You need power not your own—from God, yes, but also from others. When you get into honest, supportive community, you get to lean on the strength of others. This is essential to your recovery. The Bible says it this way: "Confess your sins to each other and pray for each other so that you may be healed."[3]

To get support, you have to "confess your sins." That's hard, because we think of our sin as the greatest enemy. Our sin has been a secret, so we'd say our secret is our greatest enemy.

No.

Your ego is your greatest enemy.

We've already looked at a saying that's as true as it is well known: "You are only as sick as your secrets." Your ability to heal from your sickness is directly related to your willingness to reveal your secrets. Don't let your ego stand in your way.

The FDF

Having a community (perhaps a church or a small group) around you is great, but I've found that the larger the group, the more difficult it is to confess. That's why I'm a big fan of having *one* fully disclosing friend (or maybe two).

A fully disclosing friend (or, as the cool kids say, "FDF") is someone who knows *everything*. You've shared all your secrets and given them permission to ask any question.

So let's get back to naked. . . .

I heard a pastor named John Ortberg talk about how the Bible says the first humans were naked. He then pointed out that nakedness is a condition that only applies to humans. I had never thought of it before, but he's right. We never say, "Look at that naked cow!" or "Look, that pig is naked!"

Only people are considered naked when they're naked. I think that's why only people wear clothes. Animals don't wear clothes. Well, there are some weirdos who dress up their dogs.*

People like to dress up their dogs, but even those weirdos would probably admit their dogs don't *need* clothes. They don't think of their dogs as naked when they're not clothed.

We only talk about humans being naked, and maybe it's because only humans have something to hide. That's what keeps us sick. That's why we need a person or two we can get naked with,† because when we get naked, we get healed.

For a couple of decades I've had a group of guys I was doing life and meeting with for weekly accountability. In the last year my little guy's group has taken it up a *huge* notch. We started doing *daily* accountability. We text each other every single night to "confess our sins to each other and pray for each other so that we may be healed." I wish I could say it was my idea, but it was my friend Mike's. He asked me to provide daily accountability for him. I agreed. After about a month I asked him if we could make it mutual. He agreed. Soon everyone in our group wanted in. I have three different guys I text every night, each about a different specific area of my life requiring accountability.

One of my areas is—yeah, you guessed it—food. I discovered I have a problem. I realized "I can't; God can." I made a decision: "Because I'm God's child, I give my life to his will . . . in this specific area of my life." I had to "ask God to help me own and release my past." I also knew, for me to get better, "with God's help, I always forgive and ask to be forgiven," so I sought to understand where, in relation to my food issue, I might have sinned or been sinned against. And I knew that to become healthy, "I stay connected to God and

---

* Look online, and you'll find weird pictures of dogs in pirate and nun costumes.
† I'm being strictly metaphorical! This book can still be sold in a Christian bookstore!

others." Staying connected to God means praying about my problem and memorizing Bible verses to create new ruts for me to fall into. Staying connected to others means finding a fully disclosing friend I can confess to and receive accountability from.

In our group, we are excruciatingly honest with each other. On a day when someone has to confess he was less than perfect, he'll typically get back a text saying something like "Thanks for being honest. Remember, what you did is not who you are. God's called you to be better than that, and you ARE better than that. Don't forget all the progress you've been making. You've got this, because God's got you!"

When I text my friend Mark about food, if I confess that my eating was less than perfect, he replies with emojis of poo. Sometimes, to make sure I understand, he'll also write, "You get poo."

You can't buy encouragement like that.

Daily accountability has been life transforming. What I've realized is that with *weekly* accountability, if I am "less than perfect" on Tuesday and Wednesday but then do great Thursday through Sunday, and my friend asks me on Monday how my week has been, I can say, "Good" and feel like I'm giving an overall honest assessment. But with *daily* accountability there's no generalizing; there's no wiggle room.

I've realized that ego used to be my worst enemy. Ego was why I wouldn't confess. But now that I'm confessing, ego has become my supportive friend. I don't want to feel embarrassed by confessing sin, but if I sin, I *will* confess it, and that helps me not to do it. Now, when I do sin, I receive the kind of grace and encouragement that makes me feel like I don't want to be the kind of person who will sin again.[‡] Or I receive pictures of poo. (I won't tell you how that makes me feel.)

Naked?

So, are you willing to get completely naked?[§]

No one gets excited at the proposition. But you're not alone, and

---

[‡] The Bible says that it's God's love (not a fear of God's wrath) that leads people to repent and live pure lives. See Romans 2:4 and Titus 2:11-12.

[§] Metaphorically! Metaphorically!

you can't do it alone. So the question is: Do you really want to get better? Do you want to heal from your hurts? Do you want to overcome that self-destructive habit?

If you do, you'll get naked.

* * *

Looking for an online community of naked people? Wait . . . that came out wrong. Don't look for that. But if you want a community of people going through this Restore *journey too—it exists! Check out TheRestoreCommunity.com and find videos featuring me (fully clothed, I promise), tons of awesome resources, and people to help you on your journey.*

I SEEK TO GET OTHERS CONNECTED TO GOD

If we've actually experienced

a path that has led us to healing and wholeness,

we certainly can't be selfish with it.

We need to get others connected to God

so they can experience a path

that leads them to healing and wholeness.

But the crazy thing is

that being selfless,

seeking to get others connected to God,

turns out to be

the best thing we can do for

ourselves.

DAY 28

ANOTHER DRUNK

BILL W. IS THE GUY who founded Alcoholics Anonymous. Bill developed the Twelve Steps with some principles he learned from the Oxford Group, a small group of friends who went to church together in New York.

Bill had successfully walked through the steps and had been sober for some time when he found himself at a hotel in Akron, Ohio. It was the day before Mother's Day, which brought up bad feelings since his mother had deserted him when he was younger. He was standing in the lobby, feeling lonely, when he realized there was a bar in the hotel. The thought hit him: *I need a drink.* Then *I'm going to get drunk.*

He was now in a complete panic. He wanted to drink but knew drinking meant death. Suddenly, another thought came to mind. *I need another alcoholic. I don't need another drink; I need another drunk. I have to tell my story to another drunk. I have to find someone who needs the help I need.*

Bill contacted a church, and the church connected him with a hopeless drunk who would become known as Dr. Bob. Bill shared his story for hours. Dr. Bob listened and then accepted Jesus. Together Bill W. and Dr. Bob went on to form Alcoholics Anonymous.

No Healing without Helping

Our sixth, and last, step is "I seek to get others connected to God."

We need to get others connected to God and on the road toward healing and wholeness for *their* sake. They need it, and if we don't tell them, who will? In that sense, seeking to get others connected to God is a selfless thing to do.

But we also need to do this for *our* sake.

What's interesting in Bill W.'s story is that he didn't go to save Dr. Bob; he went to Dr. Bob to save *himself.*

We'd expect the story to be about someone who was so grateful for his newfound freedom, so excited about the path to recovery he had experienced, that he just *had* to tell other people about it. But in that moment Bill W. wasn't grateful or excited; he was afraid and desperate, and he knew instinctively that there is no healing without helping.

Jesus said, "If you cling to your life, you will lose it, and if you let your life go, you will save it."[1] I wonder if that principle applies to our healing. If we experience the joy of healing but are selfish with it, maybe it slips out of our narcissistic grip, between our tightly laced fingers.

If we care about others *and* if we care about ourselves, we need to find "another drunk" and share the story of what God has done in our lives.

One Job

Have you seen the website you-had-one-job.com? You should check it out. It features pictures where people had just one thing they were supposed to get right but failed miserably. Like putting the "Baby" department sign above the liquor. Or packaging forks in a spoons box, or hamburger buns in a hot-dog-bun bag. Or misspelling "school" on the painted crosswalk on the road.

When you read the Bible, it's hard to escape the idea that if God has one job for people who believe in him, it's to get others connected to him.[2]

I wonder if perhaps it's not only because others need to hear about God's love but also because we need to tell it.

Most Christians don't like that idea, or at least won't do it. But it's not as intimidating as we make it sound, and it's the one thing we can't fail at. We need to serve people with God's love and then look for opportunities to talk with them about God's love.

Serve Others with God's Love

There was a front-page article in the *San Francisco Chronicle* about a metro bus driver named Linda Wilson-Allen. The reason for the article, the big news, was that she loves the people who ride on her bus. A reporter for the *Chronicle* rides that bus, and he couldn't understand what was happening on it every day. The bus driver knows the regulars, learning all their names. She waits for them if they're not at the stop when she gets there. One day the reporter watched Linda get out of the bus to help an elderly woman who was struggling with heavy grocery bags. Bus drivers don't do that. Another day Linda discovered a woman in the bus shelter was new to town. She invited her to come over for Thanksgiving.

The reporter says the regulars on her bus appreciate Linda so much that they take her to lunch during her shift break, bring her gifts, and give her use of their time-shares for vacations with her kids.

Each day when she gets to the end of her route, she says, "That's all. I love you. Take care." You probably realize this, but most bus drivers don't say, "I love you" to their passengers.

As she gets up to leave the bus so the next driver can take her spot, her passengers often break into applause.

The reporter was mystified and received permission from the

Chronicle to do a story on his bus driver. He interviewed her, asking, "How do you have this attitude?" In the article he wrote what he learned: "Her mood is set at 2:30 a.m. when she gets down on her knees to pray for 30 minutes."[3]

Turns out she's serving people with God's love.

John Ortberg, a pastor in the San Francisco area,[4] interviewed Linda at his church. He asked about her 2:30 prayer time. She said, "So we talk. I ask God to show me my life, so he shows me my life. He puts things in front of us. He could be working on my patience, or it could be someone less fortunate than I am, to give them some shoes, or whatever the case may be. . . . He'll show you. That's where my kindness comes from."

John asked her if she also prays while she's on the job, driving the bus. She replied, "Yes, when I'm out there doing my job ministering . . . I call it ministering . . . So, you see things. God will show you things. He will show you the senior who's having a hard time getting up on that coach, and how to take it in real gentle and set it down right in front of her. He'll teach you the one who's in the back who might not have all their fare, and he'll say, 'Maybe they just pay what they can.' He'll teach you these things. He just shows you. So you let your light shine that others might see your good works."

Linda Wilson-Allen is serving people in God's love, and she's doing it through God's strength.

You can do that too.

Well, maybe you can't. But God can.

Talk to Others about God's Love

If we serve others with God's love, people are going to notice. They're going to wonder. They're going to ask questions. They may even applaud. When they do, we have the opportunity to tell them our story and about the gracious God who loves us despite our junk and who has led us down a path of healing.

That may sound scary, but it's not. We're not debating with people or forcing our ideas on them or trying to make them feel guilty or wrong. We are sharing the story of what God has done in our lives and sharing that God loves them and is willing to do the same in their lives.

It doesn't have to be complicated. A simple "Here's who I was and what I struggled with. . . ." Or "Here's how I encountered God and how he's helped me. . . ."

I love the story of the guy Jesus heals of blindness.[5] The guy's pretty clueless, and his theology is dysfunctional at best. Everyone is confused at his healing, so they interrogate him, and the best answer he can give is, "All I know is I was blind but now I see. And I'm pretty sure only God could do that."[6]

Sometimes that's all the answer we need.

You can give an answer at least that good.

Well, maybe you can't. But God can.

Go

It may be the perfectionist in me, but when I see those "You only had one job!" pictures, I'm mortified. How do you fail at the *one thing* you had to get right?

It wouldn't be fair to us to say we only have one job; after all, we've walked through six steps we need to take. But we don't have any more important responsibility than getting others connected to God, for their sake *and* our sake. They need to hear about God's love; we need to tell it.

So go find someone who needs the help you need. Go find another drunk.

MOVING FORWARD

We're done!

Or maybe

we're just getting started.

If healing and spiritual growth

were a destination,

we would be done.

But since it's a journey,

we're just getting started.

So what do we need to know

as we walk out of rehab

and move forward

into the rest of our lives?

NOT TRYING

We are just about done with our virtual thirty-day rehab experience. There are just a couple of things I want to cover with you before you're "released," and I hope they'll help you when you're tempted to "relapse." The first is a reminder of one of the most important principles that will help you stay "sober." The second is more of a mindset we need to have moving forward.

The Edge of Tomorrow

For so long we've felt that living without our hurt or without our self-destructive habit was something that might happen tomorrow. Never ready to take that step, it was never today, but always, hopefully, tomorrow. Now we have the knowledge and tools we need, and so we stand at the edge of tomorrow.

Our situation reminds me of a movie. A movie called *The Edge of Tomorrow*.

Tom Cruise plays Major Bill Cage, who may look like a hero but isn't one. He is a soldier, but one who just sits behind a desk. He isn't the fighting type. In fact, he's never seen battle a day in his life. His job is more talking about it—he creates promotional videos and press releases for the military.

As the movie begins, we learn our country is at war against aliens who seem impossible to defeat. They have already conquered nearly all of Europe. A general asks Major Bill Cage to go out with his camera crew to the battlefront to show America something encouraging from the war.

Cage refuses. He doesn't do war. He doesn't go to battlefronts. He doesn't fight.

The general insists. Cage threatens him. The general doesn't receive that well, so Cage is arrested, stripped of his rank as a major, and instead of being sent to the battle as an officer on a special mission, he's sent to the front lines to *do* battle with a unit stationed at Heathrow Airport in London. Suddenly, he's just another grunt strapped into a newfangled exoskeleton weapon that he's never been trained in. In other words . . . he's a dead man. And that is exactly what happens. He goes into battle against the aliens, has no idea what to do, and is dead within five minutes.

But just before he dies, he somehow manages (by mistake) to release the safety on his gun and shoot one of the bigger aliens. Blood comes spurting out of the alien, goes into Cage's mouth, and the two of them die together.

Then . . . Cage wakes up. He was dead, but now he's alive again. And, oddly, it's the same day again. He has somehow gone back in time and is reliving the day when he was put into the unit at Heathrow Airport. Everything is exactly the same.

The only difference is Cage can choose to live this version of the day differently. He now possesses the knowledge he gained the day before to use in living the day again.*

---

* If you've seen *Groundhog Day*, it's a lot like that, except Tom Cruise instead of Bill Murray, and killer aliens instead of a shy groundhog.

He goes, again, into battle. This time he knows how to switch off the safety on his gun, and so he does a little better. He lasts about six minutes, then dies again.

Then he wakes up, and it's the same day again. Everything is exactly the same. He has to live the day all over again, except he can live it and go into battle a little better prepared because he's now practiced this day twice.

This happens, over and over and over. Five times, ten times, a hundred times—each day a new day but the same day.

Each day he has more knowledge and increased experience, and he knows what to expect in the battle. He's better equipped to fight because he's done it before, and so each day he experiences more and more success.

In the process of living the same day over and over, Cage meets Rita Vrataski. Rita is the only soldier to lead a successful surge against the attacking aliens.

Cage realizes they need to team together to experience victory against the aliens. So he starts every day by connecting with her and then goes into battle side by side with her.

Not Trying

You may be able to relate to Major Bill Cage. I know I can.

Our enemy is not invading aliens, but we do have an enemy. It may be self-defeating thoughts, or a marriage that isn't what we hoped, or an inability to stop eating or gossiping or spending or drinking or getting into relationships with the wrong people.

You have an enemy, and he attacks *every single day*.

So it's easy to just give up. Maybe you're like Major Bill Cage in that you haven't really fought a day in your whole life. You're not the fighting type. You realize, to get this problem area of your life where it needs to be, it's going to be a battle. You've got to go to the front line.

So how are you going to win the battle?

People generally think, *Well, I'll just try harder.* Right? *I know I've failed over and over, but this time I* really *want to change, more than ever before, so I'm going to try harder!*

That doesn't work. Trying harder never works, in anything, and it's not going to give you victory in your problem area. This is *not* about trying.

It's about *training.*

As we leave our stint in rehab and venture out into the real world, what's going to be different, and what will give us victory, is not trying; it's training.

This principle is true in so many areas of life, but for some reason we don't apply it to the most important areas of our lives.

Think about school. Let's say you start taking a class. You don't know anything about the subject matter. You want to get an A on the final exam. How do you get from where you are (not knowing anything about the topic) to where you want to be (an A on the final exam)? Not by trying hard when you take the test! Right?

Picture showing up at the final exam and telling the person sitting next to you, "I really want an A."

He says, "I haven't seen you in class. Have you come to class at all?"

"No."

"Oh." He seems puzzled. "Did you read the textbook?"

"No."

He's now very confused. "Have you studied at all?"

"Nah."

"Then," he pauses, mystified, "how are you planning on getting an A?"

"Oh," you smile confidently, "I'm going to try really hard."

You are not going to get an A! Why? Because you tried really hard instead of training.

The way you would get an A is by training, right? Here's a great definition of training: training is doing what I can do today so I can do tomorrow what I can't do today.

So the new semester of school starts. What *can't* I do today? I can't get an A on the final exam. Why? Because I don't know the material. But what *can* I do today? I can go to class. I can read a chapter of the textbook. I can take notes, make study cards, and read over my study cards.

Will that get me to a place where I can get an A on the final exam? No, not yet. But if the next day I go to class again, read the next chapter, take notes, make more study cards, and read yesterday's study cards, and if the day after that I do it again, and the day after that I do it again, I might just get an A.

Kind of like Major Bill Cage doing the same thing over and over, each time with a little more knowledge, a little more experience, each time getting a little better, a little closer to his goal. Going from someone who had never fought and had no skills to eventually being an alien-killing machine.

It's very similar with school. What happens is step by step, by training (*not* trying), by doing what I can do today so I can do tomorrow what I can't do today, I *will* get to a place where I can get an A on the final exam.

You read all that and think, *Duh. Of course that's true with getting an A in school.*

So what about with physical fitness? Let's say you have a goal that you want to run a marathon. Crossing that 26.2-mile finish line is where you want to be. But right now, where you are is thirty-five pounds overweight, and you haven't run since you got timed in the mile in gym class in eighth grade. You haven't exercised at all in years. Last night for dinner you had Twinkies, and for dessert you had . . . more Twinkies.

But you decide you really want to run the marathon. So you sign up for it, and the day of the marathon you show up. Before the gun goes off, the person standing next to you says hi and asks how long you've been training.

"I haven't," you tell her. "I haven't run since eighth grade."

"Oh," she says. "What's that on your shirt?"

You laugh. "Pancake syrup. Got some on me when I was eating my double stack this morning."

"Oh." She seems concerned. "Are you feeling confident you're going to be able to do this marathon?"

You smile. "Yeah, because I am going to try really hard."

She asks, "Did you say you're going to try really hard?"

"Yup!" You tell her, "Hey, could you tell me if my sneakers are tied? I have trouble seeing them, you know, past my stomach."

The marathon starts. Are you going to make it? No. After a mile or two, you'll be on the side of the road, throwing up and crying for your mommy. Why? Because you tried really hard, but you didn't train.

The way you go from being out of shape to being able to run a marathon is by *training*. What you can't do today is run a marathon, so you do what you can do—you can run a mile. Then you run a mile the next day and the day after that. Soon you find you can run two miles, then three. You run every day. At the same time, you give up on your all-Twinkie diet.* You change your breakfast plan from pancakes and bacon to egg whites and turkey bacon. You start doing push-ups and sit-ups whenever you watch TV.

What happens is step by step, by training (*not* trying), by doing what you can do today so you can do tomorrow what you can't do today, you get to a place where you can run a marathon.

You read all that and think, *Duh. Of course that's true with running a marathon.*

Here's the deal: this principle doesn't work just with getting an A in school or running a marathon; it works with *everything*. But for some reason we don't realize that, and we don't apply it to the most important areas of our lives.

One area we probably haven't applied it to is overcoming our addictive thinking and behavior.

---

* It was good while it lasted!

A Life of Training

You've wanted to get past whatever it is for a while. You've had thoughts like *I could quit if I just tried harder . . . if I had more self-discipline . . . if I loved God more.*

No.

Can a person show up for a final exam and get an A because they've tried hard? No. What if they take the test with self-discipline? No. What if they really love God? Will that get them an A? No. Only training for the test will get them an A.

You will get past your addiction not by trying hard but by entering into a life of training.

Repeatedly doing the six steps you've learned in this book is how you enter into a life of training to get past your addiction.

It's like Major Bill Cage reliving the same day, doing the same thing, but every day getting better at it and therefore making progress. It's like someone preparing for a marathon, so running every day, each day getting better at it and therefore making progress. You are going to do the six steps every day. Every day you'll get better at it and make progress.

So every day you'll train by . . .

Admitting, "I can't; God can." That's not a one-time decision; it's a way of life you enter into. Something inside you will fight against it, and you'll want to grab the reins from God and live in your own strength. But with each day of practice you'll get better at living an "I can't; God can" kind of life.

Every day *you'll decide "Because I'm God's child, I give my life to his will."* You will discipline yourself to remember who you are. You are God's child, and you are loved by him with a perfect love. As you get used to living in that, it will become more and more natural to give your life to him and his will, moment by moment.

Every day *you will "ask God to help you own and release your past."* You will practice not being a victim. Day after day you will own your issues, but you won't let them own you. It will be a challenge at first, but as you train, it will become more instinctive.

You'll train by every day *committing again to "with God's help, I always forgive and always ask to be forgiven."* With practice, you'll become quicker at forgiving, and asking for forgiveness will go from burdensome to almost effortless.

Every day *you will absolutely "stay connected to God and others."* You'll begin your day by priming your limbic brain with prayer. You'll convert your neocortex from pimp to preacher by reading and memorizing signature Bible verses. After a while, thinking God thoughts will go from feeling foreign to being second nature. What will make that easier is that you'll have some people who are partnering with you on your journey, encouraging you and keeping you accountable.

Last, *you will look for opportunities every day to "seek to get others connected to God."* Each time you share your story, you'll find that your past is losing its grip on you and that you're gaining power.

You don't overcome by trying hard; you overcome by entering into a life of training. As you do what you can do today, you'll find yourself tomorrow being able to do what you couldn't do today.

Who Is Your Rita?

One more thing about this life of training: it *really* helps if you have a Rita.

Rita Vrataski was the soldier Bill Cage hooked up with.* She had been training longer and had experienced some victories in the battle. It wasn't until Cage connected with Rita and started going into battle side by side with her that he started making significant progress.

There's a reason that when you go to a recovery group, you get a "sponsor." A sponsor is someone who has been training longer and has experienced some victories in the battle. It's someone who can share wisdom you don't have yet, encourage you when you feel like quitting, hold you accountable when you're tempted, and help you to overcome.

---

* In more ways than one.

Do you have a Rita?

If not, how could you get a Rita? Who could be your Rita? When you pray about it, who does God bring to your mind?

It doesn't have to be someone with the exact same struggle as you. It *does* need to be someone who understands and has experience with the ideas in our six steps[†] and has entered into their own life of training.

You need a Rita.

Go get a Rita.

Relapse

People who go to rehab relapse into their addictions about 40 percent to 60 percent of the time.[1]

Why? For a lot of different reasons, but one is because they focus on trying instead of training.

Don't try; *train.*

If, after rehab—or, for the rest of us, after reading this book—a person slips back into old thinking or behaviors, does that mean the rehab has failed? Does it mean the person is still an addict who hasn't really made any progress?

Not necessarily.

It means not yet.

That's the last thing we need to talk about.

[†] It doesn't have to be experience with these six steps the way I've worded them but with the basic concepts, all of which we find in the Bible and just about all of which we find in the Twelve Steps.

NOT YET

WHEN IS FAILURE *NOT* FAILURE?

When it propels you toward success.

When does failure propel you toward success?

Always.

If you let it, failure can always propel you toward success.

So failure isn't final. In fact, failure *isn't* failure.

It's just . . . not yet.

Redefining an F

In 1995, Molly Howard, a longtime special education teacher in Louisville, Georgia, applied to be the principal of the brand-new Jefferson County High School.[1]

She got the job, and she was in for a challenge. The majority of the students—80 percent of them—lived in poverty, and only 15 percent of the students who had attended the previous high school had gone to college.

Many teachers felt defeated and basically gave up on the other 85 percent.

Howard jumped into action.

She knew the students would live out their identities, so she had to help them form a new identity. She got rid of the school's two-track system that had distinguished between "college bound" and "vocational" students. From now on, *everyone* was college bound.

One of the most important changes Howard made was to the grading system. Under her leadership, the only grades the school offered were A, B, C, and NY.

"Not yet."

Howard realized the students thought of themselves as failures and accepted failing behavior. The students often didn't do their homework or turned in assignments that were unsatisfactory. They realized they would get a bad grade but accepted that as normal, and they'd be done with the work.

In the new system, unsatisfactory was unacceptable. Every student would be *required* to get an A, B, or C. If they turned in work that didn't clear that bar, instead of receiving a D or an F, they got a "not yet." They were told how to improve their grade, and they were required to do so.

The assignment they turned in wasn't a failure; it was a learning opportunity. What used to be a permanent failure was now a springboard propelling them toward success.

It changed the students' expectations, helping them to believe they could do better.

As you might guess, the school was transformed. Teachers became more engaged, students' efforts improved dramatically, graduation rates soared, and student test scores rose so much that all remedial courses were eliminated because they were no longer necessary.

In 2008, the National Association of Secondary School Principals named Molly Howard the US Principal of the Year, out of 48,000 candidates.

Growth Mind-set

What happened at Jefferson County High School?

Molly Howard gave the students what Carol Dweck, a professor at Stanford University, calls a "growth mind-set."[2]

Dweck first started noticing the difference between people with a growth mind-set versus a fixed mind-set during a study of children who were given a series of puzzles to solve. The puzzles were easy at first, and every kid solved them with no problem. But the puzzles became increasingly challenging and eventually just about impossible for the kids to solve.

Many of the children became annoyed and gave up.

Other children were not discouraged by their failure with the impossibly difficult puzzles. According to Dweck, "They didn't even think they were failing. They thought they were learning." One ten-year-old smiled at an absurdly difficult puzzle and shouted, "I love a challenge!" Others asked where their mothers could buy similarly difficult puzzles for them to do at home.[3]

Those two types of kids inspired Dweck to study those two types of approaches in all kinds of people. In her book *Mindset*, Dweck contrasts people with a fixed mind-set versus a growth mind-set.

People with a fixed mind-set believe you are what you are, your abilities are static, and your behaviors are set in concrete.

People with a growth mind-set believe you are not yet what you will be, your abilities are like muscles—built with practice—and your behaviors can be different tomorrow than they were today.

Good news: Dweck has researched whether people can change their mind-set, and they *can*. In fact, just becoming aware of a fixed mind-set can help a person move toward having a growth mind-set.

A study was done with struggling junior high students.[4] Asked why they were doing poorly in school, they offered fixed mind-set explanations: "I am the stupidest." "I suck in math."

The school was divided into two groups. One group was taught generic study skills. The second group was taught to have a growth mind-set. They were taught that the brain is like a muscle that can be developed with exercise. They were asked to think about skills they had learned (like skateboarding or mastering Guitar Hero) and to remember how hard it was to balance on a skateboard or play Guitar Hero the first time. They were taught "Everything is hard before it is easy" and that they could grow smarter and better at school.

Jimmy, one of the least engaged and worst students, asked, with tears in his eyes, "You mean I don't have to be dumb?"

Students in the control group, who were taught generic study skills, saw no improvement in their grades. Students in the "growth mind-set" group, who received only two hours of "you can change; your brain is like a muscle" training, saw rapid improvement "dramatically out of proportion with the intervention itself."[5]

Fixed mind-set kids, with only two hours of help, grew into *growth* mind-set kids.

Recurrence Is Not Relapse

At rehab you would hear a lot about relapse. Relapse happens when a person falls back into an addictive pattern after a temporary time of not engaging in it. At rehab you might learn that *many* people relapse when they go back into the real world.

Why?

Because addicts tend to have a fixed mind-set. At rehab they briefly hold on to a thread of hope that they can change, but when they experience a moment of failure, it convinces them that they were right in the first place—they *are* failures and can never really change. So they give up on their recovery and dive back into their addictions.

What's ironic is that they went through perhaps a thirty-day rehab where they didn't engage in their addictions and then lived out in the "real world" for weeks, months, maybe even years without engaging in their addictions, but one moment of giving into temptation convinced them they couldn't stay sober. Why did that brief moment of defeat outweigh the continuous string of weeks or months or years of victory? It shouldn't have, but they were taken captive by a fixed mind-set.

We're not going to be.

We're going to choose to live with a growth mind-set.

Even with our challenging issues, we are not failures, and we don't accept a culture of failure.

Failure isn't final. I'd argue failure isn't even failure; it's a learning opportunity.

When we're tempted in the old ways we used to be tempted (and we *will* be tempted in the old ways we used to be tempted) and we give in to those temptations, that's not a relapse; that's a recurrence. And a recurrence is an opportunity to grow. We can examine

- how we were tempted and what it triggered in us;
- whether we tried to overcome in our own strength or truly depended on the power of God;
- if we had primed our limbic brains with prayer that day; and
- why we had fallen into our old ruts instead of the new ruts we had established by memorizing a string of signature Bible verses.

I'm not encouraging us to screw up, but honestly, we learn a lot more from failure than success. That's why a recurrence isn't failure; it's a learning opportunity. What others might view as a sign of the permanence of our problem we see as a springboard propelling us toward success.

We are no longer standing at the edge of tomorrow, we are in it; we are living it. We now have a path out of our past, a journey of healing, and a way to wholeness.

Therefore, since God in his mercy has given us this new way, we never give up. . . .

For God, who said, "Let there be light in the darkness," has made this light shine in our hearts so we could know the glory of God that is seen in the face of Jesus Christ.

We now have this light shining in our hearts, but we ourselves are like fragile clay jars containing this great treasure. This makes it clear that our great power is from God, not from ourselves.

We are pressed on every side by troubles, but we are not crushed. We are perplexed, but not driven to despair. We are hunted down, but never abandoned by God. We get knocked down, but we are not destroyed. . . .

That is why we never give up. Though our bodies are dying, our spirits are being renewed every day. For our present troubles are small and won't last very long. Yet they produce for us a glory that vastly outweighs them and will last forever! So we don't look at the troubles we can see now; rather, we fix our gaze on things that cannot be seen. For the things we see now will soon be gone, but the things we cannot see will last forever.[6]

Until that day comes, we press on, knowing that failure isn't final. In fact, failure isn't failure.

It's just not yet.

* * *

Hey—I'm so glad you made it to the end. Seriously, I wasn't sure anyone would actually read this far. Maybe you're reading this first, just to see if you want to bother reading the rest. Let me tell you: you do.

But in all seriousness, I wanted to give a final shout-out to TheRestoreCommunity.com. If you haven't already joined, do it now. Sure, you've finished the book, but did you connect with others, share your struggles, and experience a community of people praying together for restoration? It's an incredible thing.

You'll be able to continue your journey of restoration with thirty videos that correspond with the chapters in this book and a free PDF journal that gives deeper encouragement, insight, Scripture, and reflection questions.

THE TOP TEN SIGNS YOU'RE GLAD
THIS BOOK IS OVER

10. You're running out of kindling for the fireplace.

9. You can get back to thinking of a password other than "password."

8. You have time to check on the Eggos you buried in your backyard to see if the waffle tree has grown yet.

7. You can now brag that you read a whole book since you got out of school.

6. The pizza rolls are done.

5. The bookstore is about to close.

4. You can go back to giving your ice cube collection the loving attention it deserves.

3. You have one day left before you have to return it to the library!

2. You're tired of saying, "That's just stupid" every couple of pages.

1. You're cursing Dave Letterman for inventing Top Ten lists.

The Letter I Wrote about Me, to Me, from God

(Because Obi-Wan Made Me)

Vince,

I am love. I am compassionate and gracious, slow to anger and *abounding* in love (Psalm 103:8). I showed you my love by sending my one and only Son that you might live through him. Love is not that you love me, but that I love you and sent my Son to take away all your sins (1 John 4:8-10). Therefore, there's no longer any condemnation for you (Romans 8:1). You have been set free! Not only that, but I have poured my love into your heart through the Holy Spirit, whom I have given to you (Romans 5:5). I have great love for you and I am rich in mercy, so I raised you up with Christ and seated you with him in the heavenly realms so I might show the incomparable riches of my grace, expressed in my kindness to you (Ephesians 2:4-7). So my loving you isn't about you; it's about *me*, and it makes *me* look great.

Vince, if I am for you, who can be against you? If I didn't spare my own Son, but gave him up for you, how will I not also graciously give you all things? Who will bring any charge against you, whom I have chosen? I am the one who justifies. So take joy in this: nothing can separate you from the love of Christ. You are more than a conqueror through Jesus who loves you (Romans 8:31-37)! Though you are more than a conqueror, you will still struggle. But since I am a high priest who is able to empathize with your weaknesses, who has been tempted in every way, just as you are—yet did not sin—you can approach my throne of grace with confidence, and receive mercy and find grace to help you in your time of need (Hebrews 4:15-16).

I have lavished my love on you so you could be my child. And that *is* who you are (1 John 3:1). You are my child. You are my friend (John 15:15). I like you. I like spending time with you. And I have called you to come to me, because I know you are weary and burdened, and I want to give you rest. Walk with me and learn from me, for I am gentle and humble in heart, and you will find rest for your soul. For my yoke is easy and my burden is light (Matthew 11:28-30).

So stop worrying that you aren't good enough, or doing enough. And stop striving to impress or to earn approval. Straining and trying don't help. They're a way of you staying focused on you. Instead, consider everything less important than just knowing Jesus (Philippians 3:8). Stop relying on yourself. That's religion. I have called you into grace. So rest, understanding that you can know and rely on my love for you. I am love. Live in love, and you will live in me, and I will live in you (1 John 4:15-16). Stop living in fear that you're not good enough. There is no fear in love. Perfect love drives out fear, because fear has to do with punishment. The one who fears is not made perfect in love (1 John 4:18). And though you are not perfect, my love for you *is*. So there's nothing you could ever do to make me love you less or to make me love you more.

Really, I don't care about what you do for me; I care about your love for me. I want relationship with you, which is why I have invited you into the dance. So focus on knowing Jesus (Philippians 3:10). And as you are being rooted and established in love, I will give you the power to grasp how wide and long and high and deep is the love of Christ, to know my love, that you may be filled with it and live a full life (Ephesians 3:17-18). Remain in my love (John 15:9), and do everything in love (1 Corinthians 16:14). Because the only thing that counts is faith expressing itself through love (Galatians 5:6). And live out your calling: I have called you to speak to the saved on behalf of the lost, and to the lost that they might be saved (Proverbs 31:8; Romans 15:20-21). It's fun for me to see you do what I made you to do. And remember, I am the vine; you are a branch. If you remain in me and I in you, you will bear much fruit; but apart from me you can do nothing (John 15:5).

When it comes down to it, it's all about me and my love. (Remember, I am love.) And I am bigger. Bigger than your need to make a difference with your life, to have security, or to make sure everything is problem-free. Bigger than your desires for other things. Bigger than your past or your future. Bigger than your understanding of me or your lack of understanding of me. Bigger than your sins or your achievements. Bigger than how you feel other people feel about you. Bigger than your love or lack of love for me. Bigger than the impact you make or don't make for me. It's about me and my love. It's not about you. So you can rest. You are free. So stop striving, and thinking, and worrying, and just focus on me.

In love,

I Am love.

Six Steps to Freedom

I CAN'T; GOD CAN.

BECAUSE I'M GOD'S CHILD, I GIVE MY LIFE TO HIS WILL.

I ASK GOD TO HELP ME OWN AND RELEASE MY PAST.

WITH GOD'S HELP, I ALWAYS FORGIVE AND ASK TO BE
FORGIVEN.

I STAY CONNECTED TO GOD AND OTHERS.

I SEEK TO GET OTHERS CONNECTED TO GOD.

Acknowledgments

I WOULD LIKE TO THANK:

Jesus. Because of him, God has done extraordinary things and brought extraordinary healing to my very ordinary life.

Jen. I thank God every day for giving me you. I can't imagine doing life without you.

Dawson and Marissa. Every day of my life is better because you two are in it. You are the ones Jesus loves.

The people of Verve Church and our Restore recovery ministry. It's an honor to be on this journey with you and to get to share what we're learning and our stories with the world.

The team at Tyndale, especially Ron Beers and Jon Farrar, for wanting everyone to experience the true life that Jesus makes possible and allowing me to write about it.

Tony Young and the team at City On A Hill, for your passion for Jesus and bringing his light to the world.

Don Gates, for believing in me and helping me to be able to write.

The people who read this book in its earliest phases and helped to shape it: Tim Sutherland, Kristen Lunceford, Aaron Saufley, Jennifer Antonucci, and especially Jonathan Schindler.

Notes

INTRODUCTION: REHAB . . . FOR THE REST OF US
1. Psalm 6:3.
2. Psalm 51:12.
3. Psalm 119:107.
4. Jeremiah 31:18.
5. Lamentations 5:21.
6. 2 Corinthians 13:9, ESV; 2 Corinthians 13:11, ESV.
7. Zechariah 10:6; Isaiah 57:18, NIV.
8. 1 John 4:20, NIV.
9. Colossians 3:13.
10. Matthew 6:14-15.

DAY 1: THE BLOWOUT
1. Psalm 32:3-4.
2. See Matthew 7:3-5.
3. See 1 Corinthians 6:12.
4. See Luke 8:26-33.
5. Psalm 32:5, 7, 11.

DAY 2: THIRSTY
1. Heather Kopp, *Sober Mercies: How Love Caught Up with a Christian Drunk* (New York: Jericho Books, 2013), 89–90.
2. Jeremiah 2:13, NIV.
3. Tim Keller, *Counterfeit Gods* (New York: Penguin Books, 2009).
4. Moshe Halbertal and Avishai Margalit, *Idolatry*, trans. Naomi Goldblum (Cambridge, MA: Harvard University Press, 1992), 10.
5. Jeff VanVonderen, *Tired of Trying to Measure Up* (Minneapolis: Bethany House, 1989), 124.
6. Ezekiel 14:3, NIV.
7. See Matthew 6:33.
8. Ecclesiastes 3:11.

DAY 3: A SAFE PLACE TO HIDE
1. Brennan Manning, *The Ragamuffin Gospel: Good News for the Bedraggled, Beat-up, and Burnt Out* (Colorado Springs: Multnomah Books, 2005), 25.

DAY 4: PLAYING GOD
1. See Matthew 6:25-34.

DAY 6: MY PROBLEM WITH ME
1. Romans 7:15-24.

DAY 7: DROWNING
1. Andrew Delbanco, *The Real American Dream: A Meditation on Hope* (Cambridge, MA: Harvard University Press, 1999), 24–25.
2. To read more of what my friend Kyle Idleman says about our heart problem and the inability of behavior modifications to fix it, check out his book *Gods at War: Defeating the Idols That Battle for Your Heart* (Grand Rapids, MI: Zondervan, 2013).
3. Matthew 15:19 (emphasis added).
4. Matthew 23:25-28.
5. Sister Molly Monahan, *Seeds of Grace: Reflections on the Spirituality of Alcoholics Anonymous* (New York: Riverhead Books, 2002), 2–3.
6. See John 5:1-9.

DAY 8: THE POWER I NEED
1. Roxana Hegeman, "Sheriff: Woman Sat on Boyfriend's Toilet for 2 Years," *Wichita Eagle*, March 11, 2008, http://www.kansas.com/news/local/article 1011284.html.
2. See Matthew 14:22-31.
3. See Mark 14:66-72.
4. 2 Peter 1:3.
5. Psalm 46:1, NIV.
6. Ephesians 2:1, NIV.
7. Ephesians 1:19-20.

DAY 9: CLINGING TO GOD'S LOVE
1. John 21:7.
2. Ephesians 2:1, NIV.
3. Ephesians 2:4-5.
4. Heather Kopp, *Sober Mercies: How Love Caught Up with a Christian Drunk* (New York: Jericho Books, 2013), 145.

DAY 10: GOD? OR THE STICK?
1. For the whole story, see Exodus 2–7, 14, 17.
2. See Exodus 17:8-15.
3. Exodus 17:15.

4. Proverbs 21:31.
5. Psalm 91:1-2, NIV.
6. Psalm 91:14-16, NIV.

DAY 11: WHY YOU DO WHAT YOU DO

1. Proverbs 23:7, NASB.
2. Check out James G. March, *A Primer on Decision Making: How Decisions Happen*, with the assistance of Chip Heath (New York: Free Press, 1994), especially chapter 2.
3. You can read about this study in the book by Chip Heath and Dan Heath called *Switch: How to Change Things When Change Is Hard* (Toronto: Random House Canada, 2010), 158–60.

DAY 12: I KNOW I AM, BUT WHO AM I?

1. See Exodus 2–3.

DAY 13: TRUTH FROM THE ATTIC

1. 2 Corinthians 5:17, ESV.
2. See John 15:15.
3. See Colossians 1:13-14.
4. See Romans 8:37.
5. See Ephesians 2:10, ESV.

DAY 14: CLOTHES OFF. CLOTHES ON.

1. 2 Corinthians 10:3-5, NIV.
2. Colossians 3:1-3, NIV.
3. Colossians 3:5, 7, NIV.
4. Colossians 3:9-10, NIV.
5. Colossians 3:12-14, NIV.
6. Abraham J. Twerski, *Addictive Thinking: Understanding Self-Deception*, 2nd ed. (Center City, MN: Hazelden, 1997), 25.

DAY 15: GOD ISN'T WHO YOU THINK HE IS

1. A. W. Tozer, *The Knowledge of the Holy* (New York: HarperCollins, 1961), 1.
2. See John 1:18; 14:8-9; Colossians 1:15; Hebrews 1:3.
3. See John 19:4, 7. The best the Pharisees could accuse him of is that Jesus claimed to be God, which he did. That was no sin; that was his true identity.
4. See 1 Peter 2:22; 1 John 3:5.
5. See, for instance, Matthew 8:23-27.
6. See, for instance, Matthew 7:28-29.
7. See, for instance, John 4:39-42.
8. See, for instance, John 8:1-11.
9. See, for instance, Luke 19:1-10.
10. See, for instance, Luke 23:39-43.
11. See Matthew 4:1-11.

12. See John 11:1-44.
13. See Mark 3:21.
14. See Luke 22:44; Hebrews 5:7-8.
15. See Matthew 26:37-38.
16. See Matthew 26:40, 56; Luke 22.
17. See Matthew 27:46.
18. Isaiah 53:3, ESV.
19. See Hebrews 2:10.
20. See Hebrews 2:14-18.
21. Hebrews 4:16.

DAY 16: JUMP!

1. You can find a version of this illustration in John Burke's *Mud and the Masterpiece: Seeing Yourself and Others through the Eyes of Jesus* (Grand Rapids, MI: Baker Books, 2013), 23.
2. See, for instance, James 2:19.
3. Luke 9:23.

DAY 17: OWNING MY PAST

1. For biblical examples, see, for instance, Psalm 139:23-24 and Lamentations 3:40.
2. John 8:32.
3. Michael Mangis, *Signature Sins: Taming Our Wayward Hearts* (Downers Grove, IL: InterVarsity Press, 2008).

DAY 18: RELEASING MY PAST

1. Heather Kopp, *Sober Mercies: How Love Caught Up with a Christian Drunk* (New York: Jericho Books, 2013), 135.
2. See 1 John 1:9.
3. Isaiah 1:18.
4. Hebrews 4:16.
5. James 5:16.

DAY 19: YOU HAVE TO GO THROUGH EDOM

1. You can read their stories in Genesis 25–33.
2. Genesis 32:11-12.
3. Genesis 33:3-4.

DAY 20: BUT WHY?

1. Romans 12:18, NIV.
2. Romans 12:17, NIV.
3. Matthew 5:38-39, NIV.
4. Philip Yancey, *Rumors of Another World: What on Earth Are We Missing?* (Grand Rapids, MI: Zondervan, 2003), 223–24.
5. Dana Davidsen, "Bill Clinton on Mandela: 'He Inspired Me before I Knew Him,'" *CNN*, December 6, 2013, http://politicalticker.blogs.cnn.com/2013/12/06/bill-clinton-on-mandela-he-inspired-me-before-i-knew-him/.

DAY 21: BUT HOW?

1. Ephesians 4:31-32, NIV.
2. Ephesians 4:32, NIV.
3. Lyons later dropped his lawsuit against Morice. See Leslie Williams, "Boat Owner Drops Lawsuit," *Times-Picayune*, September 8, 2006, http://www.nola.com/katrina/index.ssf/2006/09/boat_owner_drops_lawsuit.html.
4. Philip Yancey, *Rumors of Another World: What on Earth Are We Missing?* (Grand Rapids, MI: Zondervan, 2003), 223–24.

DAY 22: BUT WHAT ABOUT ME?

1. 1 John 1:9, NIV.
2. Hebrews 10:17, NIV.
3. Matthew 5:43-44.
4. Romans 12:17, NIV; see also 1 Peter 3:9.

DAY 23: TIME TO GET EVEN

1. Matthew 5:23-24, NIV.
2. Luke 19:1, NIV.
3. Luke 19:5-6.
4. Luke 19:7.
5. Luke 19:8.

DAY 24: LIVING OUT OF YOUR LIMBIC

1. Romans 8:5, NIV.
2. Romans 12:1-2, NIV.
3. 1 Thessalonians 5:17.
4. Psalm 16:8.
5. Ephesians 6:18.
6. Psalm 73:28.
7. Psalm 16:11.
8. Piercarlo Valdesolo, "Scientists Find One Source of Prayer's Power," *Scientific American*, December 24, 2013, http://www.scientificamerican.com/article/scientists-find-one-source-of-prayers-power/.
9. Kevin Rounding et al., "Religion Replenishes Self-Control," *Psychological Science* 23, no. 6 (May 2, 2012): 635–42, http://pss.sagepub.com/content/23/6/635.abstract.
10. Cited in Malcolm Gladwell, *Blink: The Power of Thinking without Thinking* (New York: Little, Brown and Company, 2005), 53–57.
11. Ibid., 56.
12. Max Lucado, *Just like Jesus: A Heart like His* (Nashville: Thomas Nelson, 2003), 63–65.

DAY 25: CREATING NEW RUTS

1. Romans 7:21-23.
2. 1 Peter 5:8.

3. 2 Corinthians 11:3.
4. See John 17:17.
5. 2 Corinthians 10:5, NIV.
6. See Matthew 4:1-11.
7. Psalm 119:11.
8. 1 Corinthians 6:19-20.
9. 1 Corinthians 6:12.
10. Matthew 6:25.
11. John 6:35.
12. John 4:34.
13. Philippians 3:19-20.
14. 1 Timothy 6:6-8.
15. Matthew 6:21.
16. Matthew 6:19-20.
17. Philippians 4:13.
18. Matthew 5:28.
19. Job 31:1.

DAY 26: RATS IN A CAGE
1. Bruce K. Alexander and Linda S. Wong, "The Myth of Drug-Induced Addiction," Department of Psychology, Simon Fraser University, Burnaby, British Columbia (summary of testimony to the Senate of Canada, 2002), last revised June 2010, http://www.brucekalexander.com/articles-speeches /demon-drug-myths/164-myth-drug-induced.
2. Johann Hari, "The Likely Cause of Addiction Has Been Discovered, and It Is Not What You Think," *HuffPost*, April 18, 2017, http://www.huffingtonpost .com/johann-hari/the-real-cause-of-addicti_b_6506936.html.
3. Lee Robins, quoted in Alix Spiegel, "What Vietnam Taught Us About Breaking Bad Habits," NPR, January 2, 2012, http://www.npr.org/sections /health-shots/2012/01/02/144431794/what-vietnam-taught-us-about -breaking-bad-habits.

DAY 27: THE FDF
1. 1 Corinthians 10:13.
2. Heather Kopp, "When Shared Brokenness Trumps Shared Beliefs," *HuffPost*, July 2, 2014, http://www.huffingtonpost.com/heather-kopp/bonding-over -brokenness-v_b_5247781.html.
3. James 5:16.

DAY 28: ANOTHER DRUNK
1. Luke 17:33.
2. There are approximately a gazillion verses we could look at, for instance Matthew 28:18-20, Mark 16:16, and Acts 1:8.
3. Sam Whiting, "Muni Driver Will Make New Friends, Keep the Old," *San Francisco Chronicle*, September 8, 2013, http://www.sfchronicle.com/bayarea /article/Muni-driver-will-make-new-friends-keep-the-old-4797537.php.

4. John Ortberg is a favorite of mine. I've read so many of his books and listened to so many of his sermons that I'm pretty sure I steal some of his ideas and phraseology without realizing it. I thereby would like to give him credit for some of the best ideas and phrases in this book, though I can't say exactly which ideas and phrases they are.

5. See John 9.

6. See John 9:25, 30-33.

DAY 29: NOT TRYING

1. See, for instance: "Drugs, Brains, and Behavior: The Science of Addiction," National Institute on Drug Abuse, last updated July 1, 2014, https://www .drugabuse.gov/publications/drugs-brains-behavior-science-addiction /treatment-recovery.

DAY 30: NOT YET

1. You can read about Molly Howard in Chip Heath and Dan Heath, *Switch: How to Change Things When Change Is Hard* (New York: Broadway Books, 2010), 173–75.

2. See Carol S. Dweck, *Mindset: The New Psychology of Success* (New York: Random House, 2006).

3. Ibid., 3–4.

4. Heath and Heath, *Switch*, 165–67.

5. Ibid., 167.

6. 2 Corinthians 4:1, 6-9, 16-18.

Top Ten Lists

Discussion Guide

OUR PROBLEM

1. Vince describes "our problem" using four different pictures: a blowout (day 1), thirst (day 2), our need for a safe place to hide (day 3), and our desire for control (day 4). Which image speaks to you in the clearest way about your problem? In what ways have you tried to address your problem? How successful have those efforts been?

2. In the introduction, Vince writes about overcoming the dysfunction of his past: "By myself, I couldn't do it. With God, I still couldn't seem to do it. But God + rehab: *boom*" (page 7). What is your reaction to the idea of a "rehab for the rest of us"? Why is rehab an important part of the equation for Vince and for you?

3. In day 5, Vince talks about the costs of going to rehab as well as the costs of not going to rehab. Have you ever thought of your issue as having costs? Why or why not? Think about your problem and take an honest assessment: What is your issue costing you?

STEP 1: I CAN'T; GOD CAN

1. Have you ever made a New Year's resolution about your problem? If so, what was the result? Was it successful? Why or why not? According to Vince, why do our resolutions so often fail?

2. Describe a time when you've felt stuck in a situation. Why was it so hard to get out of it? Look at Vince's account of the apostle

Peter (pages 71–73). In what ways does your situation of being stuck seem like Peter's? In what ways is it different? How did Peter become unstuck?

3. Vince describes a stick as "something you've looked to for help to get you past your problem" (page 92). What stick has God used in your life? What will it look like with your problem for you to prepare "the horse . . . for the day of battle" but for "the victory [to belong] to the LORD" (Proverbs 21:31)?

STEP 2: BECAUSE I'M GOD'S CHILD, I GIVE MY LIFE TO HIS WILL

1. On pages 100–102, Vince describes James March's identity model of how we make decisions. Look at some of your own recent decisions. Does March's identity model help to explain why you chose the way you did? Explain. Do you agree with Vince's statement that "what you do is determined by what you think of you"? Why or why not?

2. Vince writes, "What we believe about ourselves is largely based on what we've been told about ourselves. Humans are like sponges, soaking in those messages. Those messages form our identity" (page 108). What identity has been formed for you by the messages you've soaked in? Why do you think those messages are the ones that have stuck? Are these messages your true identity? Why or why not?

3. Vince writes that your true identity is as a child of God. What does that identity mean for you? (For some ideas, see pages 113–117.) What will it look like for you to live out your true identity as God's child?

STEP 3: I ASK GOD TO HELP ME OWN AND RELEASE MY PAST

1. Vince suggests taking a moral inventory of "habitual sins and the damage they've caused others" (see page 143). What is the

purpose of taking this moral inventory? Is it difficult to do? Why or why not? How will taking an inventory help you to "own and release your past"?

2. Why is it necessary to confess the moral inventory to God? To another person?

3. Describe a time in the past when you have confessed. How did you feel before and after the confession? How did the other person feel? What was the result?

STEP 4: WITH GOD'S HELP, I ALWAYS FORGIVE AND ASK TO BE FORGIVEN

1. On pages 168–171, Vince describes what forgiveness is and isn't. Is any of this surprising to you? Does it change your perspective on the people you need to forgive or seek forgiveness from? Explain.

2. Vince lists three steps for how to forgive (see pages 178–182). Whom in your life do you need to forgive? How might these three steps lead you to view that person and your relationship differently? Why is it important to "always remain in the role of the one who needs forgiveness"?

3. What is the difference between true guilt and phantom guilt? (See pages 188–189.) What is the purpose of true guilt? How have true guilt and phantom guilt acted in your life? Why should phantom guilt have no place in your life?

STEP 5: I STAY CONNECTED TO GOD AND OTHERS

1. What is the connection between the limbic brain and recovery? How does prayer help to prime the brain? Think of a time when you have been tempted by your problem. How did prayer help you, or how might prayer have helped you in that situation?

2. What ruts have you fallen into with your problem? What Scripture passages might help you form a new rut? Why is Scripture memorization important to overcoming addiction?

3. In day 27, Vince talks about the FDF (fully disclosing friend). What is the importance of relationships with other people in dealing with your issue? Do you currently have an FDF? If so, how has that relationship helped you in your addiction? If not, who might be a good choice to accompany you in your recovery?

STEP 6: I SEEK TO GET OTHERS CONNECTED TO GOD

1. Why is there "no healing without helping" (page 244)? How have you seen this principle in your own experiences? Why is serving others necessary to your own recovery?

2. Think of the people you know. Who needs to hear about the love and restorative power of Jesus? How can you reach out to them this week? What is your story of "All I know is I was blind but now I see" (page 247)?

MOVING FORWARD

1. How has training been effective in your life? Give examples. How might training help you with your problem? List specific steps you can take.

2. Think of how you have dealt with your problem in the past and your successes and failures. Have you had a fixed mind-set or a growth mind-set? (See pages 263–264.) How has this mind-set affected your progress? Vince writes, "Failure isn't final. I'd argue failure isn't even failure; it's a learning opportunity" (page 265). How can you learn from prior failures in order to break out of your past and into God's future?

About the Author

VINCE ANTONUCCI pastors Verve, an innovative church that seeks to reach people who work on and live around the Las Vegas Strip. The television series *God for the Rest of Us* chronicles Vince's work there. In addition to pastoring and writing books, Vince leads mission trips around the world, speaks nationwide, and performs stand-up comedy in Las Vegas. Most of all, he loves spending time with his wife, Jennifer, and their two kids.

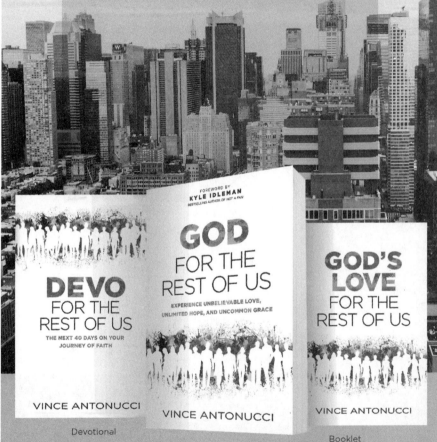

>>> LEARN MORE

WANT TO LEARN MORE ABOUT VINCE'S CHURCH FOR PEOPLE WHO DON'T LIKE CHURCH AND HOW YOU CAN PARTNER WITH THEM?

VIVALAVERVE.ORG |||| ||| |||| ||

WANT TO LEARN MORE ABOUT THE MOVEMENT VINCE'S CHURCH IS LAUNCHING TO PLANT CHURCHES IN SINFUL PLACES FOR CYNICAL PEOPLE?

||||| ||||||| **SPLAGNA.COM**

CP0952